O9-BTZ-987

ELIZABETH

Enters

THE STORY OF A QUEEN

BY
LAURIE JOHNSTON

PHOTOGRAPHS SELECTED
BY RICHARD W. JOHNSTON

PROPERTY OF
HILLANDALE SCHOOL

New York
CHARLES SCRIBNER'S SONS

921
2563

921
2563

TO DANA

COPYRIGHT 1953 BY LAURIE AND RICHARD JOHNSTON

All rights reserved. No part of this book
may be reproduced in any form without
the permission of Charles Scribner's Sons

PRINTED IN THE UNITED STATES OF AMERICA   A

❋ Contents ❋

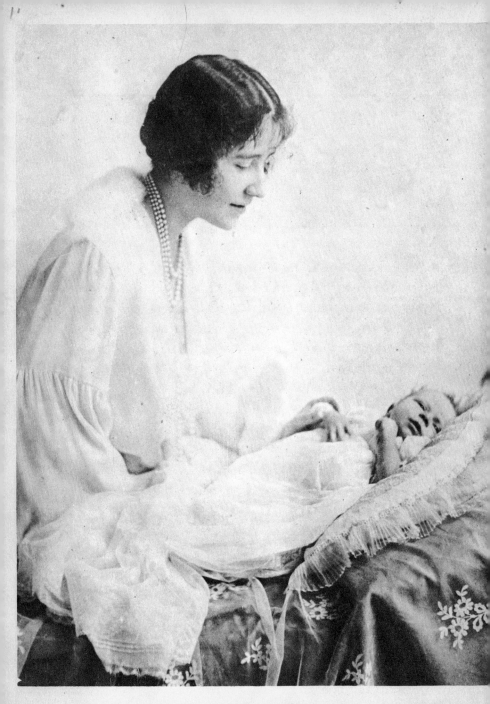

Soon after her birth Elizabeth "sat" for this portrait with her mother.

CHAPTER ONE

A Princess for Britain

ON A FRESH APRIL MORNING in 1926 a beaming London bobby paced up and down in front of a fine old house in the fashionable Mayfair section of the city. Since the night before, crowds outside the iron fence had asked him, "Is it a Prince or a Princess?"

Now the answer had come from inside the house. Rocking back and forth from heels to toes, the policeman smiled as broadly as the chin-strap on his helmet would let him. "It's a girl," he announced to each new questioner. "It's a Princess!" The word rustled through the crowd as, one by one, the waiting Londoners rushed away to be the first to tell their friends. Shouts and cheers went up from those who stayed, and a babble of excitement grew as voices talked the whole thing over.

The baby slept right through it.

Down along the Thames River the fishmongers and dockworkers cocked an ear at those who spread the news and then grinned at each other. Before long newsboys raised a racket in the streets, shouting headlines about the birth of a child. In Soho a shopkeeper sweeping off his sidewalk called to his neighbor: "Nice to have a new baby in the Royal Family, wot?" And in Piccadilly a young girl passing a flower stand

1

thought the news called for splurging a bit in celebration. Picking out a bunch of early violets, she smiled at the flower seller and said, "With the King for a grandfather, could be that baby will grow up to wear the crown." The old woman smiled back but shook her head. "Not likely," she said.

It didn't seem much more likely that evening in the fine old house in Mayfair. The baby in the ruffled crib was awake now, and making her own kind of racket to celebrate her arrival. A nurse in a crisply starched white uniform picked her up, quite without ceremony, and carried her off to her mother's bedroom.

There the young Duchess of York lay back against the pillows. The tall Duke, son of George V and Queen Mary, hovered close to his wife's bedside. As the nurse put the baby into her arms, the couple smiled at their child and then at each other. They were very much in love and now a little girl had made them happier than ever. But it was only because she was theirs — their first baby, too — and not because this bundle looked as if it might turn out to be a queen.

The baby's mother was a Scottish girl with dark hair and blue eyes. Her handsome husband was shy and boyish, with a stammer in his voice. Now his pride and excitement made him stammer even more than usual. But he managed to get out the little girl's name for the first time. "Elizabeth," he said softly, putting a big, gentle finger on her tightly curled little fist.

The Duke had named the baby for her mother more than for the Queen who had ruled England as Elizabeth I. The Duchess, before her marriage, had been Lady Elizabeth Angela Marguerite Bowes-Lyon. Her parents were the Earl and Countess of Strathmore. Their home in Scotland was Glamis

Castle, but they were not royalty – just plain-living "country" nobles.

Lady Elizabeth had been exactly the sort of sincere, cheerful, warm-hearted girl to appeal to the quiet and serious Duke – and to his parents, too. "Not one of these *modern* girls, thank heavens," Queen Mary said.

The young couple lived quietly, not caring to make a splash in social circles. They didn't even have a house of their own in London – the Mayfair home where the baby was born belonged to her Scottish grandparents. Marrying into the Royal Family had not changed the Duchess's life much, because the Duke of York was not often in the public eye.

He was a Prince, of course, which made his new daughter a Princess. He was Prince Albert Frederick Arthur George, named (like most British royalty) for nearly everybody in the family. His relatives and friends called him "Bertie." "Duke of York" was the title given him as next-to-the-oldest son of the King.

But the British crown passes to the ruler's oldest son, if the ruler has sons. And baby Elizabeth's Uncle David, the Prince of Wales, was older than her father. Uncle David wasn't married, but he was blond and gay and dashing. It seemed only a matter of time until Uncle David would marry and have children of his own, and one of them would become the heir to the crown. From the look of things, on that warm April evening in 1926, the new baby's Uncle David would be the next King and her father would be the Duke of York all his life.

* * *

The sweet voices of choir boys and the roll of organ music were the sounds Elizabeth heard at Buckingham Palace on a day in May. She was only five weeks old, but it was all in her honor. It was her christening – the baptism ceremony that would make her name official.

The christening of a royal baby, as for any baby, is a time for the gathering of the family. Royal aunts, uncles and cousins filed into the private chapel of the Palace that Sunday, as the sun shone through the stained-glass windows.

Everyone, even the small children, curtsied or bowed to bearded King George V and tall, erect Queen Mary. It was a proud day for the King and Queen. Elizabeth was their first granddaughter and the first child born to any of their four sons.

The emblem of the York dukedom is the white rose. Lying on a silk pillow, with her fuzz of pale blonde hair and her long christening dress of old ivory lace, the Princess looked rather like a little white rosebud of York.

The christening dress had first been worn by Elizabeth's great-grandfather, King Edward VII, when he was a baby. His mother, Queen Victoria, had chosen it for him. Victoria was Elizabeth's great-great-grandmother. She had ruled the British Empire for sixty-three years, from 1837 to 1901, the last Queen to wear the crown in her own right. She was a Queen who had inherited the throne herself, not one who was simply the King's wife.

Since then the long lace dress had been worn for their christenings by Elizabeth's grandfather, King George V; by her Uncle David and by her father. Someday it would be worn by Elizabeth's own children. To this family, the Windsors, who had been England's rulers for so long, it was almost as cherished an heirloom as the Crown itself.

The choir boys, wearing crimson and gold, finished their

hymns, and the organ played on softly. The Archbishop of York began to speak the words of the christening ceremony. He was one of the two highest clergymen of the Church of England.

From a golden bowl he dipped water brought specially from the River Jordan in the Holy Land. The baby stayed quiet as a mouse as the Archbishop's hand dampened her yellow fuzz and he said: "I christen thee Princess Elizabeth Alexandra Mary."

Amid a final burst of organ music, the aunts and uncles crowded round. Like all relatives, the princes, the dukes and the duchesses wanted a good look at the new baby. The Princess yawned in their faces.

No one knew then that within two years she would rechristen herself. "Lilibet" was what she chose. She found that "Elizabeth" was much too big a mouthful.

* * *

The Duke and Duchess didn't have very long to enjoy their new baby before they had to leave her for several months. The King's subjects like to have royalty make frequent public appearances, and members of the royal family share these duties as part of their job. So when Elizabeth was nine months old, her mother and father sailed away to represent the King on a visit to Australia and New Zealand, nations of the British Commonwealth that also pledge allegiance to the Crown.

Sadly they kissed their little daughter goodbye for awhile, but they left her in good hands. There were the two grandmothers to watch over her. Besides, English babies whose parents can afford it have nursemaids called "nannies." Elizabeth's nanny had been nanny to her mother, too, when the

Duchess and her brothers and sisters were little in Scotland. They had called her "Alla" because they had trouble pronouncing her first name, Clara.

So before long Alla and the baby princess moved into Buckingham Palace with the King and Queen. They had the huge garden all to themselves for Elizabeth's airings in her baby carriage—or "pram." And for weekends at Windsor Castle, the royal family's favorite country home, her highchair was set up in the Queen Victoria Tower, which had been turned into a nursery.

To this baby the Queen of England was just Grandma. She liked to chew on Queen Mary's long pearl necklace until the Queen bought her a string of beads of her own to cut her teeth on. When the first tooth came through, the King was so excited and pleased that he cabled the news all the way to the baby's parents in Australia. He was like a lot of grandfathers. You would have thought, to watch him, that his grandchild was the first baby that ever did anything so remarkable.

The old gentleman was rather stern and crusty with most people. Even his own children had always been a little in awe of him. But he adored this little girl with the pink cheeks and golden ringlets. She sat in her highchair, just as if it were a throne, and waved her spoon like a scepter, and even the King obeyed.

When she grew a little older, "Lilibet," as the King called her, liked to play with Snip, his Cairn terrier, and Charlotte, his parrot. Charlotte had been the King's pet ever since he was a young man in the Royal Navy. She wasn't in awe of the King, either. When he wasn't around and Charlotte wanted him, the parrot would make the little Princess laugh by squawking:

6

"Where's the captain? Where's the captain?"

Probably her grandfather would have spoiled Lilibet pretty badly, if he had just done what he wanted to, instead of what he thought he should. Even so, he slipped once in awhile. For her first birthday, while her parents were still on their trip, he

The Duke and Duchess proudly showed off their princess for a royal photographer when she was a few months old.

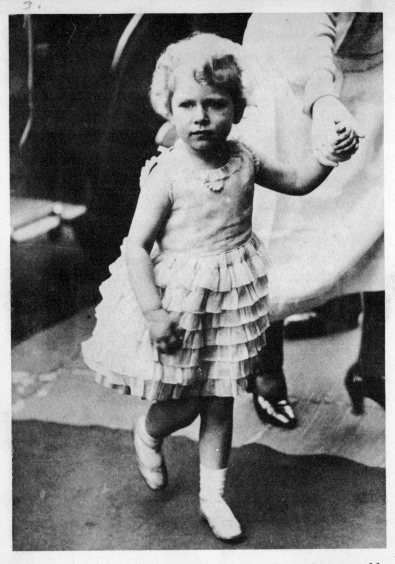

In 1929 Elizabeth was a solemn but dressy three-year-old.

gave her a dappled white and gray rockinghorse. He got so excited about the horse that it never occurred to him that Lilibet wasn't old enough to ride it.

But Grandpa was also the King, and the little Princess soon got her first glimpse of the pomp and pageantry that would fill so much of her own life. A crowd of Londoners, waiting outside Buckingham Palace, saw Alla hold the baby up to a window and pull the curtains back. There below, Elizabeth could see her grandpa and grandma, wearing robes of ermine, driving off in a magnificent procession of horse-drawn carriages to the opening of Parliament, while the crowd cheered.

* * *

The Princess had learned to say her first word, "Mummie," to her mother's picture. Now, however, the Duke and the Duchess came back from their long trip and the little family moved into a home of its own. Their new address was 145 Piccadilly, just a step from Hyde Park.

It wasn't very fancy compared to Buckingham Palace, but it was a tall, stone house in a fashionable part of the city. It was old, but it had been redecorated inside so it would be comfortable and attractive. It had a garden at the back for Elizabeth to play in, and a nursery on the top floor. Alla came along and moved into the nursery with "her" baby, and there were several servants.

Now the Duke and Duchess were back, they wanted to settle down with their little girl to a quiet family life. They wanted her childhood to be just as normal as if she were not a princess.

That was hard to arrange. Elizabeth was just a year and a half old, but already the London newspapers were talking about how much attention she was attracting. More attention, they said, than any other royal baby had ever received. Some of the newspapers were so eager to write about her that they didn't always bother to be accurate. Her father started a scrapbook of clippings that he jokingly titled: "Things That Never Happened to Us."

Plenty of things did happen, though. If the little girl appeared in public wearing yellow, London stores immediately advertised toddlers' clothes in "Princess Betty Yellow." Just before Christmas Lilibet came out dressed all in holly red, clasping a large doll dressed just the same. London mothers rushed to outfit their little girls in "Princess Betty Red."

Everybody at Buckingham Palace, too, made a great fuss over Lilibet. Even the stately Queen Mary could unbend when her grandchild was around. Once when the Princess was having lunch with the Queen, a Salvation Army band played a serenade outside a palace window. Queen Mary invited the leader inside, and Lilibet wanted to know all about his cornet. When he finally got back to his band members, what a story he had to tell them! The Queen of England, he said, took the cornet and marched across the room playing an imaginary tune, to the delighted giggles of her granddaughter.

For her second birthday Uncle David, the Prince of Wales, had given Lilibet a Sealyham puppy. For her third, he gave her a Cairn terrier puppy. Her fourth birthday was one of the best of all. Uncle David sent his present all the way from Africa, where he was hunting. (Luckily, he didn't try to send another puppy from there—it might have been grown up by the time it arrived!) Her mother and father gave her a tricycle and Queen Mary gave her a Noah's Ark full of tiny animals, two by two.

To have a proper birthday party, the whole family had gone out to Windsor Castle, one of the country estates owned by the King. But for awhile it seemed to Lilibet that Grandpa must have forgotten all about getting her a present. Pretty

A birthday present for Lilibet arrives at Windsor Castle.

soon, though, he took her by the hand. "Let's take a walk, Lilibet," he said.

They went down to the royal stables, where the Princess already had made friends with the horses and the grooms. Suddenly she spied something new—the birthday gift the King had hidden there—and Lilibet went wild with joy. It was one of the smallest Shetland ponies he could find, her very own to keep there and ride around Windsor Great Park, part of the castle grounds.

That same day she found out just what she meant to the British people. Her grandfather liked to take her with him when he went driving or to make appearances, so the public was used to seeing the little girl, in bright coat and leggings, skipping down the red carpet that had been laid for the King. Always there were cheers for her as well as for him.

But on this fourth birthday, at Windsor, she appeared alone to watch the changing of the guard. Actually, "changing the guard" simply means that one group of soldiers guarding the Castle goes off duty, and another group comes on. But the British make a colorful ceremony of this change; whether at Windsor or Buckingham Palace, a band plays and there is a lot of saluting and marching up and down by soldiers in handsome uniforms. This usually draws a crowd of onlookers, and that was the case on Lilibet's birthday. As the tiny fair-haired girl in primrose yellow walked across the quadrangle, the crowd cheered wildly and rushed closer in spite of watchful police. The crush of people was so great that the huge gates of the Castle had to be closed.

Princess Elizabeth sensed that this time it was all for her. Shyly she waved her hand, and then blew a kiss to the crowd. This brought on even louder cheers.

Clearly she was the pet of the public as well as the pet of the family. You can see how the little Princess could almost have begun to think the whole universe centered on her. It was a good thing another baby was on the way.

If it turned out to be a little brother, of course, the spotlight of attention would be focused on him instead of her. A boy, though younger than Elizabeth, would move ahead of her as possible heir to the throne. If a baby sister arrived, Elizabeth would still have some chance of being Queen. But her country and her family would have two little princesses to adore instead of just one.

That summer Lilibet and her parents went north to the

cool Scottish moors. They often went there to vacation at historic Glamis Castle, the home of Grandmother and Grandfather Strathmore.

The four-year-old Princess couldn't read but she liked to look at pictures. One day she went in to the nearby village with her mother to buy a book, proudly carrying her own new purse. As the clerk showed her one book after another, she examined and rejected a great many. "I've seen that already," she would say.

Finally she found one that was new to her, asked the price and made her decision. "I'll take that," she said. Then with great dignity, she produced her purse and paid for her purchase herself.

On the night of August 21, 1930, a summer storm broke over the moors. Thunder and lightning played above the massive walls of Glamis Castle, the ancient home of Macbeth. While a swirling rain fell outside, the new baby was born.

It was a little sister for Lilibet. In London the news was told again. And in Glamis village and far out across the drenched moors, bonfires were lit to celebrate the first birth of a Royal Princess in Scotland in more than 300 years. To the Scots the little Duchess of York was their own and they loved her even more when they learned the new Princess would bear the good Scottish name of Margaret Rose.

Soon Lilibet would have someone to play with in the nursery, someone to share the dapple-gray rockinghorse with, and the picture books and the romping with the dogs. But if she sat upon the throne, it would not be her sister's to share. And Princess Elizabeth was nearer to it now than on that April day when she was born.

The "lady of the house," HRH Princess Elizabeth, pauses on her doorstep.

CHAPTER TWO

A Little House of Her Own

DID YOU EVER WISH for a little house all your own? Not a dollhouse, but one just big enough for girls and boys? A house with its own miniature silverware, a real telephone and radio, lights that switch on and off, a kitchen full of equipment, and a shining bath?

Most little girls might as well dream of being a princess as dream of ever having such a house. But Elizabeth of York already *was* a Princess. The people of the British Empire would give her many a beautiful home during her lifetime, and on her sixth birthday the people of Wales gave her the first one, tiny but real.

It was thatched like a Welsh cottage but it was two stories high—living room, kitchen and hallway downstairs; bedroom and bath upstairs. It stood in its own garden plot on the grounds of Royal Lodge, the Duke and Duchess of York's own country home on the grounds of Windsor Castle. Over the door a plaque told its name: "Y Bwthyn Bach" (Welsh for "The Little House").

On that first Saturday morning after workmen had finished getting it ready for her, Lilibet was too excited to eat much breakfast. Out of the family's big house she skipped, up the tiny stone walk across the cottage lawn, to unlock her own front door for the first time.

Like another Goldilocks, she tried all the chairs in the pine-paneled living room. They were all "just right," she found, hugging herself with delight. Halfway up the curving stairway, on the landing, a little desk held an invitation to write her first letter—stationery and blotters with her royal crest. Upstairs in the tiled bathroom, bright with mirrors and chromium, Lilibet turned the tiny faucets and found that the water ran hot and cold.

Down on her knees before the linen closet, she fingered the towels, sheets and table linens, all hand-embroidered with a crown and the initial "E," and the soft woolly blankets.

How could Lilibet decide what was the most wonderful thing in the house! Everything "worked." And everything, even the gas stove and the white refrigerator in the kitchen, was just the right size for a little girl, instead of that giant-size furniture that grown-ups make for themselves and then expect children to fit.

Immediately the Little House was Lilibet's favorite plaything. What fun to have tea parties there, with nobody invited who couldn't stand up under the 4 foot 8 inch ceilings!

One Saturday her cousins, George and Gerald Lascelles, were coming to Windsor with their mother, Princess Mary, for the weekend. Lilibet was a conscientious housekeeper, so she went out to the Little House early to get ready for her guests. How would you imagine she went about it? We don't know exactly but we can suppose . . .

She pulled back the gay chintz draperies in the living room to let the sunshine in. With her little broom and carpet sweeper, she went to work on the pretty rug in the living room and the carpeting on the stairs. She dusted the "antique" furniture. She put flowers in a Wedgwood bowl on the mantel under the painting of Mummie in a blue dress that matched her eyes.

In the blue and white kitchen she looked over the small containers of flour and baking powder, sugar and spices, and wondered if she should try baking a cake for tea. She looked at the rolling pin and pastry board, and was torn between a cake and a tart. "Golly," the family cook, let her help sometimes and had promised to teach her so she could really cook in the Little House.

But today perhaps it might be safer just to toast muffins for tea. Opening a cupboard stocked with canned goods in miniature, Lilibet rather felt like giving her guests a full meal. But she decided on just canned fruit—and some of that good cheese with the muffins.

With Margaret Rose scrambling to keep up with them, the boy cousins soon arrived—ravenously hungry, in the usual manner of males. The little sister ran joyously from room to room, squealing over each new discovery and picking up everything that wasn't fastened down. She never could get enough of the Little House, especially since she wasn't, as yet, allowed to play there regularly.

George and Gerald admired everything dutifully, too, without letting themselves be carried away by the sights. They were more interested in Lilibet's food. They hardly seemed to notice the old-fashioned glass flowers and the needlepoint panels that Lilibet was so proud of. They were enormously fascinated, though, by her little telephone and all the plumbing fixtures and electrical appliances, and even the miniature insurance policy. When they left, contentedly full of food, Lilibet knew her party had been a success.

She cleared the Spode tea service away to the kitchen, looking a little regretfully at the Spode dinnerware and the cheerful set of breakfast dishes, all still on their shelves. It was rather a pity they hadn't got all the dishes dirty at once, it was such fun to wash them in the lustrous pewter sink!

When the dishes were dried and the glassware shiny as soap bubbles, Lilibet wrapped up the gleaming silverware (as she did every week-end before she left for London), to keep it from tarnishing. Then the small housewife, a bit tired by now, glanced at the model-sized grandfather's clock. She knew Mummie would be expecting her at Royal Lodge—but she could hardly bear to leave her own little home. Not, anyway, without one last tour of inspection.

Up in the bedroom, under the curving eaves of the thatched roof, Lilibet sat herself down in front of the dressing table, with its blue chintz skirt. She fondled her monogrammed silver brush-and-comb set, and gave her hair a pat or two. Then she yawned.

The Tudor oak bed, with a spread of blue chintz, looked very inviting. Her doll was already fast asleep in a tiny cradle with bedclothes that matched Lilibet's bed. The little Princess lay down for just a moment, to think about her successful tea party. And that's where the Duchess found her, fast asleep, when she came looking an hour or so later.

❋ ❋ ❋

By now Lilibet was going on seven years old, and Margaret Rose was a bouncy two. It didn't seem long since that Scottish summer when she was born in a rainstorm, and to her sister she often seemed about to flood England with her own rainstorm of baby tears.

Sometimes Lilibet thought everybody paid too much attention to this little creature who had come to live with her and Mummie and Papa. When she had something very interesting to talk to Papa about, and Margaret Rose would interrupt by climbing all over him, Lilibet wondered why they hadn't left her in Scotland.

But other times it was worth it. Having someone younger in the family made Lilibet feel rather like one of the grownups. She liked to help Alla push the baby's pram around Hyde Park, chattering to her nanny about how "their" baby com-

While another nursemaid pulls, Alla and Elizabeth keep a firm grip on Margaret's pram as it rolls through Hyde Park.

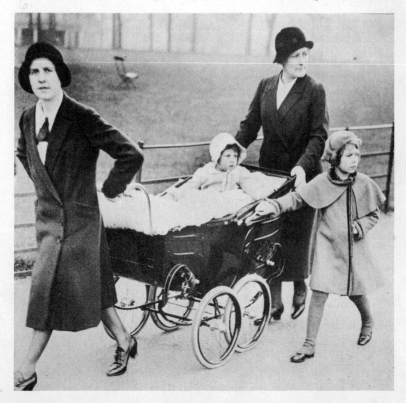

pared with the others out for airings. Often she would run across the soft grass to pluck a clover or a bright leaf for Margaret Rose.

After tea, with Margaret Rose bathed and tucked away in her crib, Lilibet would sit on the cherry-red carpet in front of the fire while Alla rocked and knitted and told stories about "when Mummie was a little girl." The Princess liked to hear about Mummie's childhood, but she was almost as much interested in "Jemima Puddleduck." Jemima was the heroine of a book, one of the first books Lilibet learned to read. Her mother had started teaching her her ABC's when she was just five.

Lilibet had other accomplishments, too. She could do a graceful court curtsy, to greet her grandparents properly as King and Queen. And she could talk French. Mummie had begun teaching her *that* when the little girl had barely learned to speak in her own language.

* * *

Almost every Friday afternoon the Duke of York's family drove off for a country weekend at Windsor, which is only twenty-five miles from London. Windsor Castle had been the home of English monarchs for more than eight hundred years. Now the King and Queen lived mainly at Buckingham Palace in London, but they usually spent their weekends at Windsor, too. The castle, with its turrets and battlements, stood on a low hill overlooking the winding River Thames, the town of Windsor and the green countryside.

Driving out from London, Lilibet could see from miles away the huge Round Tower in the center of the castle. By looking at the flag that flew from the tower, she could tell whether Grandmother and Grandpapa had arrived. If they weren't there

In this aerial view of Windsor Castle, you can see St. George's Chapel in the foreground and the Round Tower at the top, center.

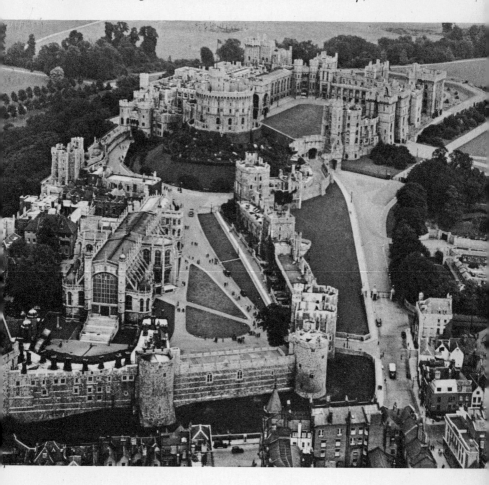

yet, the British flag, the Union Jack, would be flying. As soon as the King and Queen reached the grounds, the soldiers stationed at Windsor would hoist the Royal Standard, the special banner of the royal family, over the tower.

Arriving on Friday afternoon, Lilibet would pay her Little House a brief visit and perhaps decide whether on Saturday she would clean house or invite Margaret Rose to a tea party — or both. Then, right away, she would change into breeches and a tweed coat and race out for her riding lesson with Owen, the groom from her father's stables. She had started the lessons before she was six. She had a real riding pony now, a prancing animal she could hardly keep from hugging around its sleek, warm neck.

With her short legs sticking nearly straight out in the stirrups, Lilibet and Owen would ride the paths through the timber of Windsor Great Park, all that was left of the once vast Royal Forest. At first a bridle linked her pony safely with Owen's horse. She and the groom had long discussions about saddles, gaits and how a horse likes to be treated.

At night, before she settled down for sleep in the pink-and-beige nursery, at Royal Lodge, Lilibet tied the cords of her dressing gown to the bed posts and played she was driving a team. One night, galloping gaily on the bed, she was so surprised to see a strange face in the doorway that she dropped her "reins." Her visitor was a young woman, tall and slender, with short brown hair and a warm, friendly smile. It was Lilibet's first glimpse of Miss Marion Crawford, who had come to be her governess.

Mummie and Papa and Queen Mary had decided it was time Lilibet, now almost seven, got started at real lessons. But they felt that no school could teach her the special things a Princess, and perhaps a future Queen, would have to learn. Besides, they thought if they picked one girls' school all the others might feel slighted.

Many English children are taught at home by governesses, if their parents are well-to-do. Lilibet's father remembered some of the stiff and stuffy tutors he had had as a boy. He insisted on hiring someone who would be young enough and lively enough to be some fun for Lilibet, and for Margaret Rose, too.

Marion Crawford was twenty-three years old. She was a Scottish girl who had been an honor student at the University of Edinburgh. She had been giving lessons to Lilibet's cousin, in Scotland, when the new job was offered to her.

"Crawfie," as Lilibet soon was calling her, had a merry disposition, but she could be firm when necessary. It didn't take Lilibet long to decide that she liked her. For one thing, Miss Crawford didn't expect her to stay as clean as Alla did.

When Lilibet and Margaret Rose went out to play in the garden behind the house at 145 Piccadilly, Crawfie came right along and joined their games. They played hide and seek in the shrubbery, or ambushed each other like wild Indians. If the shrubbery was sooty, as it usually is in a big city, Crawfie would get her face just as smudgy as the little girls did.

The Princesses weren't allowed to play with many other children, but there were a few who came to visit. Two of their favorites were their young cousins, George and Gerald Lascelles. Lilibet found it quite hard to understand why these two grandchildren of the King were not Princes. Her mother explained that it was because they were the children of the King's daughter, not the children of one of his sons. Besides the Lascelles, the Princesses' playmates included the children of Lord and Lady Allendale, who lived next door, and Mummie's nephews, John and Andrew Elphinstone.

From the time she was little, Elizabeth liked to play with her cousin Gerald.

When any of the boy cousins left for home, Lilibet would watch them sadly from the window and say, "I *do* wish we had a brother." She found it hard to believe that some little girls thought having a brother had its drawbacks. It seemed not to matter to her, if she thought of it at all, that if she had a brother she would almost certainly never be Queen.

The Duke, who hadn't many duties these days, often joined the noisy games with Crawfie and the little girls. His daughters were proud of how fast he could run. He was very good at hop-scotch, too.

The back garden was right next to Hyde Park. Whenever Lilibet and Margaret Rose were outside playing, people lined up on the other side of the fence to watch them through the bars. The Princesses hardly noticed. They were used to being stared at, wherever they went, as something special.

Lilibet, naturally, rather enjoyed the way everybody seemed to think she was so wonderful. Riding with Alla and Margaret Rose, in the open carriage the King often sent to take them for a drive, she would beam and graciously wave her hand to the pleased crowds. The royal footmen, sitting up behind her in fancy uniforms, could hardly keep their faces straight.

Queen Mary often took Lilibet with her when she had to appear at meetings or social events. One such time the little girl was being naughty and fidgety and talking too much, and Grandmother threatened to take her out the back door and home. Lilibet, who had seen the crowds gathered to watch the Queen and her grandchild arrive, smiled complacently and said, "Oh, but you can't do that—all those people waiting outside to see me will be so disappointed."

You can imagine about how long it took for Queen Mary to hustle her out of there—and by the back door, too.

The Duke and Duchess took Lilibet to her first circus when she was seven. Nobody in the audience knew they were coming and not many knew they were there until a clown spotted the Princess. His name was Whimsical Walker. He was more than 80 years old and famous as the oldest clown in England.

In his funny, gaudy costume Whimsical shambled up to the royal box and shoved a "red hot" poker toward Lilibet. She only laughed merrily and grasped it in her outstretched hand. The glow of red paint on it hadn't fooled her at all. Then, with her chin on her hand, she watched spellbound as the wild animals and the performing dogs and ponies went through their acts. But the eyes of many others in the audience strayed often to the Princess herself—sure to be, wherever she was recognized, the main attraction of the day.

But if the grownups at 145 Piccadilly also adored Lilibet and Margaret Rose, they were determined to bring them up right. Alla made sure they brushed their clothes and hung them up and put their toys away when they were through with them. Mummie read stories from the Bible to the little girls, and taught them Psalms in the Scottish versions she had heard as a child.

Sometimes when the Duchess read fairy tales about Princesses who got everything they wished for and always "lived happily ever after," Lilibet would point out, "But I'm a Princess, too." Then her mother would remind her that she was a real-life Princess, and that real-life Princesses had duties that fairy Princesses never dreamed of.

And Miss Crawford, Lilibet found, could take the education of a Princess as seriously as Queen Mary, who had proud old-fashioned ideas about what should be expected of royalty. Both the elderly Queen and the young governess wanted the Princesses to grow up with something in their heads besides the public's cheers.

With the approval of the Duke and Duchess, they soon had Lilibet learning about arithmetic (her hardest subject), history (her favorite), geography, grammar and literature.

❋ ❋ ❋

Lilibet's day started at 7:30 with breakfast in the nursery with Alla and Margaret Rose. The nursery in the town house

The Princesses were enthralled by the horses and clowns at Olympia circus.

was on the top floor, and so was Lilibet's room—she had her own now—and Miss Crawford's, too. The doors all opened onto a landing under a big glass dome that let the sunlight come right in and reach clear to the bottom of the stair well.

The landing was a playground, and it was a "stable" too. Lined up around it were two or three dozen toy horses, some on rockers, some on wheels and some on four little hooves. Hardly a birthday or Christmas passed that somebody, buying a present for Lilibet, didn't decide, "When in doubt, give her a horse." Every night, for years, until the Princesses got too busy with real horses, each toy horse had his saddle removed, was thoroughly curried and got a chance to nibble from a pan of oats and take a good-night drink of water.

In the mornings, too, the horses required quite a bit of care to get them ready for the day. Then the little girls went downstairs to their parents' room for a half-hour or so, before Lilibet started her school work at 9:30.

There wasn't a regular schoolroom, so Miss Crawford and her pupil worked in a sitting room just off the big drawing room. It had pretty Chinese paper on the wall and was fitted out with desks, blackboards and maps. At 11 o'clock they took a recess for "elevenses," an English custom almost as popular as afternoon tea. Margaret Rose joined them for orange juice and crackers and then they all went out to play for an hour in the garden.

At noon they came in for an hour of rest. Margaret Rose was supposed to take a nap then, only sometimes she just played possum. Lilibet curled up somewhere and was allowed to read a book for a half hour. Then Crawfie read to her for another half hour from some of the great books that were a little harder going.

Lunch was at 1:15. Lilibet and Miss Crawford had it downstairs with the Duke and Duchess, off simple place mats painted with flowers or birds. Margaret Rose lunched upstairs with Alla. She usually finished first and then scampered down to join the others.

There were lessons in the afternoon, too. One day a week it would be dancing. Sometimes the Duke and Duchess joined in the strenuous English square-dances called reels, or the

Scottish reels that made them all wish a bagpiper were on hand to play them right.

On Tuesdays the Princesses would go off to a singing class at the Countess of Cavan's home. On Wednesdays and Thursdays, drawing and piano teachers would come to 145 Piccadilly.

Even indoors the girls spent a lot of time on horseback.

Both little girls liked music and they did well at it. Nothing pleased their father more than to have them play and sing duets for guests—especially since he had always found it so hard to perform, or even make a speech, in public. Lilibet loved her piano lessons and picking things out by ear. But she hated to practice. What was the fun of playing the same things over and over again!

At five o'clock came tea, highspot of the day in England. Like most youngsters there, the Princesses made a real meal of it. Then for an hour or more they played rummy or other card games with Mummie and Papa until, around 7 o'clock, Alla called "Bathtime!" first for Margaret, then for Lilibet.

Some days there were guests for tea. One who came most often was Uncle David. Often he brought a book as a present. He was a whiz at the girls' favorite game, "racing demon." You had to be very fast, snatching up the cards in a regular frenzy. Trying so hard to beat Uncle David, Lilibet and her sister would end up flushed with excitement or dissolved in an attack of giggles.

The Princesses' bedtime romp with their father and mother usually began when both little girls were in the bathtub. The squeals made it sound as if the Duke and Duchess might be playing with two pet seals they kept in the bathroom. Afterwards there would be pillow fights with everyone getting rosy and tousled.

When Alla called a halt, the Duke and Duchess went downstairs to their dinner. The Princesses were supposed to be in bed by 8:15, but they didn't always stay put. Some nights they would remember that they hadn't finished bedding down all the horses outside on the landing. They would pop from under the covers and run out to wind up their "stable" chores.

Another night there might be dinner guests, most of them well known in political life or society. Lilibet and Margaret Rose would huddle together at the top of the stairs where they could look down and watch the famous guests leaving their coats with Ainslie, the butler. Many of them, of course, the little girls already had met. They had their favorites, those they thought looked "nice" or "fun" or were handsome and dashing.

Others were stuffy and most unattractive, they decided, whispering secretly what Princesses—and certainly a Queen— would never be able to say in public.

At the Richmond Horse Show in 1934
Princess Elizabeth strokes the nose of a large but friendly prize-winner.

CHAPTER THREE

Horses, Holidays and History

DURING THOSE QUIETLY HAPPY YEARS at 145 Piccadilly in London and at Windsor's Royal Lodge, some of the Princesses' best friends were animals. The Duke and Duchess had always liked dogs, and the family had a lot of them. At Windsor it kept Lilibet racing to divide the weekend hours among the latest batch of puppies, the Little House and the stables.

Even in town Lilibet couldn't get enough of what you might call "horseplay." She had some red reins, with jingling bells, and she loved to "harness up" a tea guest and drive the visitor around the room or the garden. But usually Miss Crawford was the horse! She has told the story of how Lilibet used to jerk her to a stop, pat her and give her a nourishing nosebag while the Princess "delivered groceries" at imaginary houses. Sometimes she would whisper, "You must pretend to be impatient, Crawfie. Paw the ground a bit!" And Crawfie, that wonderful playmate, would paw. She found out Lilibet could be a pretty good horse herself. The little princess would prance and toss her head, whinny and nose in Crawfie's pockets for sugar.

Sometimes when other children came to visit they would all take the toy horses down to the garden from the upstairs landing. There they would have a horse market, eyeing and poking the animals critically as they raised each other's price bids. Or Lilibet, remembering what she had seen at the circus, would organize a mock "horse act." Everybody would be horses except the one who was It, who stood in the middle as ringmaster, cracking the whip to drive the galloping horses around and around.

Lilibet took her turn, like everybody else, at being It in all the games. She was being trained in the courtesy and good manners that people expect from Princesses, even when they are little. Playing with her younger sister, too, was good practice in not being selfish.

Margaret Rose wasn't a baby any more but a blonde little girl who looked rather like a smaller copy of Lilibet—only her hair wasn't as curly, unless Alla curled it for her. "Wait for me, Lilibet!" she would pipe out shrilly a dozen times a day, her short, chubby legs pumping along in an effort to keep up. Lilibet got angry sometimes, for Margaret seemed to want everything that *she* wanted.

But most of the time she could understand that little sisters are like that because they're little sisters; someday they'll be bigger sisters. So Lilibet became quite motherly about Margaret Rose—upset when she was naughty and proud when she behaved nicely. The younger girl (Princess II, as some people thought of her) never was as earnestly concerned about doing the right thing as her sister was. She knew she could get away with many things, while people expected a great deal of Lilibet.

Margaret loved to mimic anybody who struck her as funny. Lilibet didn't always think this was kind or even very amusing, and if she didn't, she said so. She could be quite critical of someone else's behavior. Her mother and Miss Crawford found, though, that if you showed her where she herself was in the wrong she was eager to correct her faults.

You can see that, though the Princesses looked so much alike and usually were good friends, they were very different girls and were bound to have their battles. Lilibet sometimes

At a garden party the Princesses help tighten the ropes on a tent.

used her fists, while Margaret Rose found biting and scratching very effective. Both had tempers, but Margaret's was quicker to flare and quicker to cool. Lilibet would boil a long time, inside, before she let it show.

Crawfie let the girls do their lessons outside when the weather was nice. They studied in the back garden at 145 Piccadilly or on the lawn of Royal Lodge when they were at Windsor. Sometimes they even did their before-breakfast daily dozen out in the sunshine. Each Princess had a pair of small-sized "dumbbells" to swing to the commands of a special phonograph record. This was Papa's idea. He was a firm believer in physical training. He hadn't been very strong, as a boy, and had worked hard to build himself up with exercise.

Learning other things could be fun too, Lilibet found out. She didn't like geography much at first. Then she began to realize that Grandfather, whom she sometimes called "Grandpapa England," also was King of all those pink-colored countries and colonies on the map—and, it just could be, someday she might be their Queen. Stories and gifts Uncle David and other royal relatives brought back from overseas trips helped, too.

Lilibet and Margaret Rose loved the country and spent a lot of time there. Even in the city they had a table-top "farm" of toy animals, tractors and buildings they had bought at Woolworth's (going there to shop with Miss Crawford was one of their greatest treats). Besides spending nearly every weekend at Windsor, the family usually went there for an Easter vacation and stayed to celebrate Lilibet's birthday on April 21. Windsor Great Park was a fine place for riding bicycles as well as ponies, and for long walks, too. Lilibet and her sister made a sort of game out of knowing the names of wild flowers and

Elizabeth and Margaret make their dogs "speak" for a tidbit.

trees and the call each kind of bird made. Miss Crawford helped them fix up a bird feeding station on an outdoor table, with a bell the birds rang as they flew in to get the food. When the little girls heard the bell, they knew they had bird guests for dinner.

Summers they all went up to Birkhall, in Scotland. Balmoral Castle was the Scottish residence of the King and Queen. Birkhall, the Duke of York's place, nearby, was much smaller. It was quite a simple home, whitewashed on the outside, with oil lamps and oil stoves to heat it on cold evenings. In wet weather Lilibet and Margaret could play on the front porch that Queen Victoria had added to the house when she used it.

Inside, Birkhall was furnished almost exactly as Victoria had left it, with the heavy, dark wood furniture that came to be known as "Victorian" because of its popularity in her day. Old-fashioned china pitchers and wash basins were in the bedrooms.

Bagpipers from the village sent the old Scottish tunes skirling, weird and sweet, through the clear, still Highland air. Lilibet—even if she wasn't born in Scotland like Margaret Rose—proudly sported a kilt. Through her father and grandfather, too, she was entitled to wear the bright red-and-yellow Royal Stuart plaid. The modern British royal family is the House of Windsor, but their blood line reaches back to the Stuart kings of Scotland who ascended the English throne in 1603 and ruled for a hundred years.

Before they left Scotland in the autumn the family would pay a visit to Balmoral Castle to stay with the King and Queen and to Glamis Castle to see Grandfather and Grandmother Strathmore. They liked to take the pony cart and drive into the village railway station with Miss Crawford, to watch the fast train from Aberdeen go by.

❋ ❋ ❋

Every Christmas the King and Queen and their children and grandchildren all gathered at Sandringham House. This was a 15,000-acre royal estate in Norfolk. Lilibet's great-grandfather, Edward VII, had bought it while his mother, Victoria, still was Queen and he was Prince of Wales. He didn't get to be King until he was sixty years old.

The Duchess and her daughters emerge from the great door of Glamis Castle.

But weeks and even months before they went there for the holidays, Lilibet and Margaret would start the busy buzz of getting-ready-for-Christmas. They painted their own Christmas cards and made some of their gifts themselves and huddled in corners together whispering Christmas secrets. They drew up their card lists and shopping lists early, with Lilibet taking great pains to help her little sister with hers.

They wrote long, confidential letters to Santa Claus. Mummie took them to see the Christmas decorations and the toy displays at a big London department store and they usually bought a few presents there.

But they did most of their gift shopping at Woolworth's. With Crawfie they would roam the store, picking out a china dog or a piece of costume jewelry or pages of bright pictures to paste in scrapbooks. They wrapped their packages and hid them with much giggling and sh-sh-sh-ing, getting particular fun out of keeping Crawfie guessing about what they had chosen for her.

The wrappings weren't always brand new. Lilibet was a regular little squirrel about putting things away for a rainy day. When it came time to dress up the Christmas packages, she could reach into a big carton she kept and pull out ribbons that had been on candy boxes or bouquets, paper lace and all the pieces of gaily tinted paper she hadn't been able to bear throwing away. She and Margaret were just as thrifty about quite a few other things. Their pencils, for instance—they used them right down to the nub. The whole royal family, in fact, saved things generation after generation, just in case. They had plenty of attic space in all those big houses!

In the exciting weeks before the holidays, the cooks in the royal kitchens were stirring up Christmas puddings and cakes and candies. Lilibet and Margaret loved to go down and "help" them, sniffing the luscious, sweetly spicy smells and doing a little tasting on the side.

Christmas Eve they hung up their stockings, Margaret Rose wondering wistfully if hers would ever be as big as Lilibet's. Then they snuggled down in bed, squirmy and shivery with excitement. When Mummie and Papa were sure their little girls were asleep at last, they filled the hopeful stockings and laid out the bigger presents. They always hung up for the girls, too, a couple of those "stockings" of stiff net you buy in stores, bulging with knicknacks—candy, a whistle, a puzzle, a doll's paper parasol, a little red rubber ball.

Sometimes Christmas morning brought one wonderful, costly present—for Lilibet, perhaps a race horse from the royal stables or a gold-headed, initialed riding crop from Uncle David. But most of their presents were things like games and books, a doll, a pretty bookmark, or a box of chocolate peppermints, Lilibet's favorite candy.

❊ ❊ ❊

Birthdays too brought family celebrations. Since they were nearly always at Windsor for Lilibet's, she liked to play hostess at a tea party in the Little House, just for Margaret Rose and the young cousins. The day she turned nine years old, though, she blossomed out as official hostess on a larger scale.

Easter holiday crowds liked to come to watch the changing of the castle guard on Lilibet's birthday. On that date, from the time she was four years old, she usually appeared to "take the salute" of the guardsmen. Her father and mother, as well as the King and Queen, thought it was good experience for her.

On her ninth birthday the guardsmen's smartly stepping military band played her a serenade. Five thousand spectators, standing outside the big gates, saw Lilibet appear alone at a castle window. Most of them lost their hearts to "the Empire's darling" right then and there. As the bandsmen tootled and thumped, Lilibet beat time on the windowpane, clapped her hands and danced up and down to the music.

Nine candles, on a pink and white frosted cake, gleamed behind her in the castle's Oak Room. There, as the bells of the castle chapel pealed in her honor, Lilibet sat at the head of the table, presiding as hostess to King George, Queen Mary, her mother and father, and a dozen or so uncles, aunts and other kinfolk.

The newest aunt at the birthday party was the beautiful young Duchess of Kent. Lilibet and Margaret Rose could hardly take their eyes off her; they thought—and they were quite right—that she had such style and wore such beautiful clothes.

The new Duchess had been Princess Marina of Greece until a few months before, when she married the Duke of Kent. He was the youngest and handsomest son of the King and Queen. At their wedding Lilibet had been the youngest bridesmaid, with a frock made for her by Norman Hartnell, the famous British designer. It was frothy white tulle over a silver slip, and she wore a wreath of white camellias. When she walked proudly up the aisle of Westminster Abbey, Margaret Rose—who was sitting near the aisle with her mother—tried like anything to make her laugh. But Lilibet looked right through her little sister. After the wedding reception at Buckingham Palace, Lilibet scooted across the Palace courtyard and pelted the bride and groom with rose petals as their carriage drove away.

13

Ermine is a royal fur, and that's what Lilibet wore at one wedding where she was a bridesmaid.

That summer Lilibet went to her first royal garden party at the Palace. These are huge affairs, with three thousand or more people invited. The guests include distinguished foreign visitors, outstanding athletes and professional people, workers who have accomplished something special, as well as the cream of British society. The King and Queen and their family move around through the crowd, saying a pleasant word here and there.

The little Princess, dressed up more than she liked to be and wearing a hat (something she hated to do), felt rather lost and confused in the great crush of politely murmuring guests. Then, from a distance, old King George spied her. His eyes lighted with pleasure and he immediately crossed the wide lawn and bent down and kissed her. Lilibet made him a perfect curtsy, as the crowd buzzed with approving comments.

The King adored Lilibet the growing girl as much as he had Lilibet the baby. But she had less time to be a sort of plaything for him, now that she was busy with so many kinds of lessons. He and the Queen, though, still took her with them often when they made public appearances.

* * *

England, like the United States, was going through "the Depression" in those years—a time when business was bad, thousands of people were out of work and suffering real hunger, and the country had problems that seemed almost impossible to solve. As a King who reigned but did not rule (Parliament really makes the laws for Britain), Grandfather couldn't do very much but show up in places where the misery was most severe and look sympathetic. With the King and Queen, Lilibet visited "benefit" parties and concerts, held to raise money

44

Elizabeth liked to go driving with "Grandpapa England" and Queen Mary.

for the unemployed. She went with them into slum neighborhoods like Limehouse where the desperate people lined up to receive free bread and soup.

Even in places like that the people—with a strange lack of envy of her good fortune—seemed to brighten up just at the sight of the little Princess.

The King was worried about the sad state of his country, and he had never completely recovered from a serious illness of his own. He was tired and he was 70 years old and his family suddenly was deeply aware of it that Christmas of 1935 as they gathered at Sandringham. It was not until January, however, that the nation heard the news in an official radio announcement: "The King's life is moving peacefully to its close." He had stayed on at Sandringham and his last, weak words told something of what it means to wear a crown and wear it conscientiously. "How is the Empire?" he asked.

Lilibet and "Uncle David" were good companions.

Lilibet and Margaret were at Royal Lodge, Windsor, when "Grandpapa England" died at Sandringham. With Miss Crawford they went to London, wearing black coats and black velvet tams. Five-year-old Margaret was too young to really understand what had happened but Lilibet, nearly ten now, was sad and pale.

All London was hushed by the pageantry of a King's funeral. Papa felt that even Lilibet wasn't old enough to go through the whole long ceremony but he wanted her to have some memory of it. So she and Crawfie went to see the King's coffin pass by, borne on a gun carriage and draped with the Union Jack, while bands with muffled drums played the slow, somber, minor harmonies of funeral marches. It was a depressing ordeal, and a tiring one too, but the little girl knew she must play her part in it. Without tears and without complaint she went through it like a Princess.

It hurt to think she would not see again the King whose eyes, above his stern and bearded jaw, twinkled with affection when he saw her. But Lilibet understood that grandparents must pass along and a new generation must take their place. She would miss King George V, but what could be nicer than having dear, delightful Uncle David as the new King?

Probably now he would settle down and start a family of his own, choosing a wife from among the many titled young women who were just waiting for him to make up his mind which one of them was to be Queen of England. Nothing would please the British people more than for the King himself to give them an heir to the throne. And for Lilibet, it would be fun to have another little cousin in the royal family.

When they donned the Coronation robes and crowns one day in 1937 the Yorks from 145 Piccadilly became the Royal Family of Britain.

CHAPTER FOUR

A Curtsy for Papa

IT DIDN'T WORK OUT that way at all.

Uncle David *was* proclaimed King, of course. He took the name of Edward VIII, and plans were begun to hold his coronation in May of the following year, 1937. But before long the little Princesses sensed that something strange was in the air — something they really didn't understand.

When they took drives through the London streets they could see black headlines and posters on the newsstands: "THE KING AND MRS. SIMPSON" or "CONSTITUTIONAL CRISIS." Uncle David dropped in to see them much less often. When he did, he looked worried and unhappy.

That autumn important men in the government and in court circles came in the door of 145 Piccadilly more often than ever. The Princesses hung over the railing of the stair landing and tried to figure out just what it was all about. Then, on December 10, 1936, they got the answer: Uncle David was giving up his throne to marry Mrs. Wallis Warfield Simpson, who could not be accepted as Queen. That was partly because she was an American, and not "royal." Mostly, though, it was because she had been divorced, and her two former hus-

49

PROPERTY OF HILLANDALE SCHOOL

bands were still living. As part of his job, the King is the head of the Church of England, and the church doesn't approve of divorce.

The British people had loved Uncle David, both as Prince of Wales and King. Now, after a little over ten months on the throne, it was all over. The King spent a last evening with his mother, Queen Mary, and his sister and four brothers at Windsor Castle. From there he made a farewell broadcast. To the whole world Uncle David declared that he found it impossible to go on with his duties "without the help of the woman I love." The King said his decision had been made easier by the "sure knowledge" that his brother, the Duke of York, could immediately take his place. ". . . he has one matchless blessing," Uncle David added, "enjoyed by so many of you and not bestowed on me—a happy home with his wife and children." In conclusion, he said: "And now we all have a new King. I wish him, and you, his people, happiness and prosperity with all my heart. God bless you all. God Save the King."

Such a thing had never happened before in all the thousand years of British monarchy. The English people were used to having adventurous Uncle David topple off fast horses, but for the King, by his own choice, to topple off his throne—! In America a lot of people sided with his decision to give up all for love, but in Britain many thought that he had taken the easy way. They felt he owed his country something for his privileged life. Now he was throwing away the supreme privilege of all—to serve it as King.

The abdication shook the whole nation, from Buckingham Palace right down to the shopkeeper in Soho and the flower seller in Piccadilly.

On her twelfth birthday Elizabeth went riding with Margaret and the King.

It shook Elizabeth's own little family most of all. For overnight her shy, gentle father was changed—as the next oldest brother—from Prince Albert, Duke of York, to King George VI. On December 12, 1936, two days after Uncle David's farewell speech, four trumpeters sounded a fanfare from the crimson-draped balcony of St. James's Palace. The royal Kings of Arms and Heralds stepped out to proclaim Elizabeth's father "our own lawful and rightful Liege Lord, George the Sixth, by the Grace of God, of Great Britain, Ireland, the British Dominions beyond the Seas, King, Defender of the Faith, Emperor of India."

It was hard for the girls to believe, as Papa left 145 Piccadilly that morning, that when he came home to lunch he would be all these new things. And that wasn't all. It suddenly occurred to Lilibet and Margaret that now they would be going to live in Buckingham Palace! In alarm and distaste they looked at each other, and then around the familiar rooms where they had been so cozy and happy. When a family friend, Lady Cynthia Asquith, came to call that afternoon Margaret burst out: "Isn't all this a bore? We've got to leave our nice house."

To the visitor she poured out other objections—she didn't like the idea of signing her name simply "Margaret," in the fashion of Kings and Queens and their immediate families. "I had only just learned how to spell York—Y-O-R-K," the little girl complained, "and now I'm not to use it any more." As though she felt that losing half of her name meant losing half of herself, Margaret went on, "Since Papa turned King, *I* don't seem to be anybody at all!"

As usual, Elizabeth was more self-controlled, but trying to hide her excitement left her big-eyed and restless. She couldn't keep from running to the window to look out at the crowd that had gathered. "*Thousands* of people outside," she reported in a wondering half-whisper.

When she saw Lady Cynthia downstairs to the front door, a letter lay on the hall table. Her expression grew solemn as she read the address on the envelope: "Her Majesty the Queen."

"That's Mummie now, isn't it?" Lilibet said, and her voice trembled a little.

Papa came home to lunch a King, looking taller than ever in his naval uniform with the rank of Admiral of the Fleet. Lilibet and Margaret swept him a court curtsy, just like the one they had always made to their grandparents, the old King and Queen. It startled Papa a little; things were changing almost too fast for him, too. Then he leaned down and gave them each something to show that he was still Papa, in spite of his big new job, and they were still his little girls. He gave them the same old bear hug and kiss.

❋ ❋ ❋

In all the excitement, and with Christmas coming on besides, Lilibet hardly thought about the chance that she might be Queen someday. She was now next in line for the throne, of course—but a little brother still might join the family. If he did, he would become Prince of Wales and "heir apparent." By custom in nearly all kingdoms, it is "apparent," or understood by everyone, that the first son of a reigning King will inherit the throne, no matter how many older sisters he has. A princess who is the nearest heir to the throne is called "heiress presumptive." That means it is "presumed" that she will succeed her father—but as long as he lives it is officially considered possible that he might have a son.

Britain's ten-year-old "heiress presumptive" lost little sleep over her new title, and its future possibilities. She was thinking more about all the new homes she would have to get used to: Buckingham Palace, Windsor Castle, Sandringham and—in Scotland—Balmoral Castle. Lilibet thought she would never like them as much as 145 Piccadilly, Royal Lodge and little Birkhall.

She especially felt this way about Royal Lodge, where her own Little House stood close by in the gardens and ponies could be ridden right up to the front steps. One of the first requests the new King had to act on was Lilibet's plea that the family should still spend its week-ends at Royal Lodge instead of Windsor Castle. He made the promise and kept it, though the decision caused a good deal of surprise in Court circles.

The family went down to Sandringham for Christmas as usual, but it was a strange gathering. For the first time there was no "Grandpapa England" and no Uncle David, and everybody was calling Mummie and Papa "Your Majesty." The new year found them back at 145 Piccadilly, but not for long. The King and Queen moved into Buckingham Palace, to get started on all the things that had to be done. (Queen Mary had moved to Marlborough House, a smaller but still handsome residence nearby that also belonged to the royal family.)

For the time being Lilibet and Margaret stayed on in their own familiar home with Miss Crawford and Alla and some of the servants. Sometimes they went over to the Palace for tea or to snoop around and see how things were going. It was hard to stick to the routine of lessons and early-to-bed, especially when big packing crates began to appear all over the house and the movers backed their trucks up to the front door.

Lilibet and Margaret deeply admired the way these strong men juggled the heaviest sofas and cabinets around as if they were doll furniture.

Long before the Princesses had to say a last goodbye to the nursery-landing and the mounted policeman on the corner outside the front door, they had forgotten their sorrow at leaving and could hardly wait to join Mummie and Papa at Buckingham Palace. Finally the great day came, February 18, 1937.

✳ ✳ ✳

Have you ever thought about what it would be like if you lived in a Palace? For most of us, of course, it would be the height of luxury in many ways—being waited on hand and foot, with hundreds of rooms to wander among and vast, well-kept gardens to play in.

But living in a Palace, as the daughter of a King, can cut you off almost entirely from life as it is lived by ordinary people. Lilibet's parents had always tried to keep her childhood as normal as possible. Even so, it couldn't help being "special." And now, in spite of their efforts, it was going to be even more fabulous—as fabulous and, in its way, as unreal as that of any story-book princess.

Outside Buckingham Palace there are black and gold railings to keep the public from coming too close. They are a symbol of the barrier—the kind you can't see—that separated Princess Elizabeth from contact with everyday folk. Inside the railings Lilibet's new home was a great, gray stone structure with 690 rooms!

The original Buckingham House was built more than 200 years ago for the Dukes of Buckingham. King George III bought it as royal property in 1762—just 14 years before the United States became a nation by revolting against him. The Palace has been remodeled many times. By the time George VI and his family moved in, it covered a city block, with four wings or sides surrounding a courtyard in the hollow center.

From the outside Buckingham Palace looked like an office building or, perhaps, a rather elaborate hospital. Inside, Lilibet and Margaret thought, it was like living in a museum. They had visited their grandparents there ever since babyhood, but they still hadn't seen it all. So now, whenever they had a chance, they slipped off to do some exploring.

The miles of dim and drafty corridors made them feel like whispering and tiptoeing, and at first Margaret often held tight to her sister's hand. Their own ancestors watched them, looking down from huge oil portraits on nearly every wall. It gave them a rather spooky feeling to remember that Queen Mary had got lost in the Palace soon after she moved in.

The furnishings in the Palace suggested a very large and grand antique shop. Generations of British kings and queens had left their treasures in the "state" apartments, where royalty entertains on formal occasions. The King and Queen were entertaining at tea one day when a lady sat down elegantly in a graceful antique gilt chair. As Lilibet and Margaret watched round-eyed, the chair fell apart with a crash. Neither they nor their parents so much as smiled. Princesses must learn early not to laugh when the joke might embarrass someone else.

If the state apartments were full of the past, the present soon brightened up the "private apartments." These were the family's real home. Five rooms had been turned into a nursery "suite," and the first thing the Princesses did after they unpacked was to line up their stable of toy horses in the corridor outside their rooms. The horses stayed there until after Lilibet was married.

It upset the children at first that their nursery and bedrooms were so far from Mummie's and Papa's. Queen Elizabeth pointed out the bright side of that: if the long halls were a nuisance in some ways, they would give the little girls more space than they'd ever had before to play in! Besides, they wouldn't be alone at night—Alla would sleep in Margaret's room and Lilibet would share her bedroom with Margaret "Bobo" MacDonald, the Scottish girl who was her personal maid.

Before long the Princesses were racing up and down the red-carpeted halls as if they'd lived there forever. Two of their favorite dogs, Dookie and Jane, raced right along with them, to the amazement of Palace staff members or visitors.

The Queen had the family's rooms done over in a homey, informal style and fresh, airy colors—robin's egg blue or cream walls with light woodwork and carpets and pretty pastel chintzes for draperies and upholstery. Mummie would have liked to turn the decorators loose on some of the state apartments too, but she didn't want to have them all torn up for the Coronation.

Now that Papa was King of England, Elizabeth had a new home—historic Buckingham Palace in the heart of London.

Everybody's thoughts and plans now centered around that great event. Actually, of course, Papa had been King ever since Uncle David abdicated. The Coronation wouldn't change anything, but it would give everybody a chance to celebrate the fact that a new King was now on the throne.

The Coronation was still scheduled for May, 1937, so there wasn't much time. Lilibet and Margaret had been looking forward to it happily when it was Uncle David who was due to be crowned. Now that it was Papa's Coronation, and Mummie's too, the girls were almost beside themselves.

In their new roles, they would play a bigger part in the ceremony itself and in the weeks of semi-official events that went with it. These started in March when the King and Queen gave their first Buckingham Palace party. In matching frocks of dusty rose, Lilibet and Margaret stood with their parents at the top of the curving Grand Staircase to receive the guests. Mummie and Papa were proud when many of the visitors praised the Princesses' good manners and friendly dignity.

The British people were catching the Coronation fever, too. Crowds of them gathered constantly outside the Palace, where the gateways opened onto the wide avenue called the Mall. Lilibet's and Margaret's rooms faced the Mall. Oftener than the crowds knew, as they looked up at the Palace windows, the two Princesses would be looking right back at them from behind the curtains. They were as curious about what people are really like as people are about princesses.

Queen Elizabeth was so busy with dressmakers, portrait painters and party arrangements that she had to give up her afternoon nap. Sometimes as the dressmakers fitted her Coronation wardrobe, she would stand for hours until nearly ready to drop. The King, looking in frequently from his study, would bring her cups of hot, strong tea to drink without sitting down.

One day Mummie was trying on the gold-embroidered ivory satin gown she would wear for the Coronation ceremony. Lilibet bounced in breathlessly. She insisted that her mother come "at once" to look at a huge box that had been delivered a few minutes before. "Can't you wait a minute, darling?" the Queen asked. Lilibet shook her head. "No," she said, "I can't wait one minute."

The Queen hastily gathered up her train and followed Lilibet to the King's bedroom, where the box had been placed. Just as the Queen reached it, a figure popped out of the top like a real-life jack-in-the-box, followed by a little brown dog. It was Princess Margaret and Dookie! They had been in an even greater hurry than Lilibet, and had burrowed down through the tissue coverings to get first look at the priceless purple velvet and white ermine of the King's Coronation robe!

Lilibet and Margaret had to stand still for the dressmakers too. As the daughters of the King, they were both to wear purple velvet and ermine miniatures of their parents' robes. Lilibet's, though, was to have a little train, to trail out behind her as she walked down the aisle of Westminster Abbey. When six-year-old Margaret heard her mother tell the dressmaker: "But Margaret needn't have a train, of course," she came close to having a tantrum.

"Oh, but I *must* have a train!" the small Princess stormed, with outrage in her eyes and voice. She wouldn't hear of having the robe stop at the floor. In the end, she won. Her train lay only 18 inches along the floor, somewhat shorter than Princess Elizabeth's, but it made Margaret gloriously happy.

Both sisters also were to wear coronets, like the other ladies of royalty and the nobility. Theirs would be even more like little crowns, with crosses and *fleurs-de-lis*, because they were the King's daughters. When they first tried them on, Margaret couldn't resist clowning a little. As she strutted around, her coronet slipped down until it was tilted across her nose. It made her look like a mischievous angel with its halo askew.

They were going to wear their first long dresses, too— creamy lace with little silver bows down the front. They would be only ankle-length, though. The Queen refused to go along with the old custom of putting royal children into sweeping gowns for Coronations. She thought they would be busy enough managing the trains of their robes without tripping over too-long dresses.

Unlike Margaret, Lilibet had never been very much interested in clothes, and even Coronation dressmaking bored her after awhile. She was much more interested in some of the other preparations that were going on.

The little girls had already found the Palace stables, with their glittering harness room, an enchanting place to play. They had "tested" the springs of every coach and carriage by bouncing up and down on the seats. Now they discovered that the horses themselves were being tested, to see how they would behave in the noise and confusion of the Coronation processions.

At first the Princesses and Miss Crawford would climb a ladder and take turns peeking through a window to watch what was going on. Stablehands were waving flags and banners in front of the horses' quivering nostrils, and a brass band played for all it was worth. Red-uniformed "soldiers," really stuffed dummies, moved back and forth on little trolleys. This was to get the horses used to noise and bright flashing colors, so on the great day they wouldn't rear and bolt.

The Princesses would have loved to be closer to all that

hullabaloo, but they were a little shy about asking. Then someone discovered them on their ladder perch and invited them inside. After that the little girls and Miss Crawford all "helped"—yelling, running up and down and waving their handkerchiefs. They'd been in enough processions to know how the people would act.

When the royal family came back to London from their Easter holiday at Windsor, lilacs and tulips were flowering in the parks and Coronation decorations were blooming out all over the city. Flags and bunting and coats-of-arms streamed from lampposts and across shop fronts. Pictures of the King and Queen and his daughters were everywhere. Business streets were in fancy dress, and even the poorer parts of town boasted home-made paper frills.

Hammering could be heard at all hours, and the Princesses watched with excitement as "bleachers" were built along the Mall outside the Palace and on down the route to Westminster Abbey. Families were trooping into London from all over the British Isles. Some had tickets for the great show and some only hoped to catch a glimpse of some part of it. More than two hundred thousand visitors were in the city—20,000 of them from the United States. As the day drew near the crowds grew, filling the streets day and night to see the sights and cheer lustily when any royal car appeared.

Meanwhile, Lilibet and Margaret were learning what they were expected to do at the Coronation. While the King and Queen took part in the long ceremony at the altar of Westminster Abbey, the Princesses were to sit with aunts, uncles and cousins in the Royal Box in the balcony. But to get there they would have to walk the length of the Abbey's center aisle, before thousands of eyes.

Over and over again they were rehearsed by Queen Mother Mary and Princess Mary, the King's only sister. The ancient ritual seemed to the little girls rather like a glorified royal wedding, though they had been taught some of its historic importance. Both of them had carried bride's trains in the Abbey. Now they were learning to manage their own.

* * *

Hardly anyone in London, it seemed, slept through the night before May 12, the Coronation Day. To be sure of seeing the procession, some people spent all night on camp stools. At dawn 30,000 soldiers from all over the Empire, wearing their dress uniforms, took positions along the route of the procession to help police keep the crowds in hand. Faces filled every office or hotel window, balcony and rooftop along the way. Even in the United States families got up in the darkness and tuned their radios—for the first time in history a description of the whole Coronation day was to be broadcast.

By 5 A.M. Lilibet, shivering with cold and excitement, was jumping in and out of bed to hear the bands play and watch the people pouring into the bleachers along the Mall. Buckingham Palace bustled with guests and their servants, but the King and Queen took time for their usual morning visit with the little girls. Then they drove away in their golden coach drawn by eight gray horses. The Princesses followed.

To the million people who lined the procession route and cheered them wildly, the blonde little girls in their white lace and royal robes looked just as Princesses should. Like Cinderella herself, they rode in a "glass coach" with big windows all around. With them in the coach were their aunt, Princess Mary, and their thirteen-year-old cousin, Viscount George Lascelles.

He was one of the six boys who were going to carry the King's 30-foot train. Margaret was so little she had a specially built-up seat in the horse-drawn carriage to allow her to see and be seen by the crowds.

When they reached the great Abbey and were helped down from the carriage, the little girls looped up their robe trains over their left arms as they had been taught. They picked up their skirts—and the crowd was delighted. Underneath all that finery their legs were bare, as usual, above their ankle socks.

A misty sun filtered through the stained glass windows of the Abbey, where more than 7,000 persons waited. The his-

On their way to the Coronation the King and Queen ride in a golden coach.

toric church glowed with lighted tapers, flowers, gold altar utensils and the jewels of spectators. Titled gentlemen, officials and members of Parliament were in court dress—satin knee breeches, velvet capes and buckled shoes. The ladies wore pale satins embroidered with gold; white feather plumes nodded in their hair.

Above this magnificence the music of the great organ, now sober, now joyful, rose to the lofty ceiling where the delicate stonework was like gray lace.

Seven thousand pairs of eyes watched as the two Princesses started down the long, long aisle. First, though, Elizabeth adjusted her little sister's train—and nearly pulled it off. Then, side by side, they walked down the rich blue carpet. From every side came whispers: "Don't they look sweet?"

A little later a hush settled over the vast assembly as Queen Mary made her entrance. She, too, wore purple velvet robes, with a diamond coronet that sparkled in her white hair. She looked every inch the Queen she had been to Britain for twenty-five years—and just as proud of her second son as she had been of her husband the day she was crowned with him.

Once in their seats, between Queen Mary and Princess Mary, Lilibet and Margaret tried to see everything at once. Queen Mary looked through her lorgnette at the printed program and explained to them what each part meant. Margaret stood on her tiptoes a good deal of the time, whispering excited questions. Other times she yawned and squirmed, for a Coronation is a very long ceremony. It contains the music, Bible scriptures and prayers of a religious service. It has other rites in which the Archbishop of Canterbury anoints the monarch with holy oil and hears his promises of faithful service. Finally, the Archbishop presents him with the time-honored signs of

22

At the Abbey Lilibet picks up her train—and shows her ankle socks!

British kingship: gold spurs, the sword and shield of Edward III, two jeweled scepters and the King's Ring.

As the three-hour service moved through its traditional steps, Lilibet and Margaret looked down more and more intently at their father. He was far from them, and from the vast congregation. He was even far from the Queen, who had always been so close to him. He seemed a lonely figure in spite of the glory all around him. His shoulders were bowed by the heavy robes, and he looked pale. The Princesses, Lilibet especially, knew that their shy, somewhat awkward father would much rather not have been King.

That was why there was a special dignity and bravery about him at that moment when the Archbishop placed on his head the gold-and-pearl St. Edward's Crown. It had been used in the Coronation of every British sovereign since the year 1661; Lilibet knew she herself might wear it someday. Watching her father, the young Elizabeth knew more in that moment than she had ever known before about courage, self-discipline and the sense of duty. She saw that these qualities could turn an everyday sort of person into a leader the nation could count on for service and example.

The lights in the great Abbey had been dim through much of the ceremony. But as soon as the crown was taken from the altar and placed on the King's head, the lights went up amid a blare of trumpets, a roll of drums and a glad burst of music from organ, orchestra and choir. King George VI mounted his throne, then, and the Archbishop presented him to the people to receive their homage.

The Queen's crowning was next. Her crown had been made specially of platinum, set with diamonds from the royal collection—among them the large and famous Koh-i-noor. At the moment the Archbishop placed it on the Queen's head, the little Princesses proudly put on their own coronets. All over the Abbey there was a rustling sound of silk garments in motion—the peeresses were adjusting coronets on their brows, too. Some of them got them on a little crooked, Lilibet noticed.

23

As thousands cheer the new Royal Family, Elizabeth waves in reply.

As the great ritual drew to its majestic close, Lilibet and Margaret suddenly realized they were hungry. The Princesses just managed to snatch a couple of sandwiches laid out in a side room for people taking part in the ceremony. Then they were on their way home, driving with Queen Mary through tossing seas of waving, cheering people. It was past four o'clock before they reached the Palace—more than six hours after they had left it to go to the Abbey.

They were tired little girls, but their duties were not finished. Photographers were waiting to take pictures. And over and over again, thunderous cheers called the whole family out to the balcony to wave and smile at the crowds in the Mall.

The King had left St. Edward's Crown at the Abbey. It is used only for the Coronation. It weighs five pounds and can't be worn with comfort more than a few minutes at a time. Now he was wearing the Imperial State Crown, which he would use for state occasions. Though it weighs less than half as much as the Coronation crown, it is set with 2,783 diamonds, 277 pearls, 16 sapphires, eleven emeralds and five rubies. One ruby is as big as a hen's egg.

The jeweled crown fascinated Lilibet and Margaret. It was like bringing the Coronation home with them. It had been a day they would talk about for months, and remember all their lives.

CHAPTER FIVE

At Home in a Palace

FOR ELIZABETH AND MARGARET the end of the Coronation marked the beginning of a new kind of "normal" life. But for all children of their generation, the "normal" world was a troubled one. In the sunshiny summer of 1937 the Princesses were dimly aware that a good many places were less happy and peaceful than their own pleasant home at Royal Lodge.

In Italy a short man with a jutting jaw and the odd name of Mussolini was strutting around like a new Roman emperor. Far off in China people were being killed by Japanese soldiers. Not so far away, in Spain, a bloody civil war was being fought, and just across the English Channel from Britain a onetime army corporal named Adolf Hitler was screaming at the German people. His motto was: "Today, Germany; tomorrow, the world!" In most of the nations people were telling themselves hopefully that the world was not going to blow up in the violence of total war. But even the most cheerful of them could hear the firecrackers going off all around the edges.

For eleven-year-old Lilibet and six-year-old Margaret, the biggest problem was how to come down out of the pink clouds they had been walking around on since before the Coronation. King George, Queen Elizabeth, Queen Mary, Miss Crawford, Alla—everybody agreed firmly that the Princesses must now "settle down."

Elizabeth was growing up and beginning to care more about her appearance. When she looked in the mirror she could see, like most little girls, that some things about her were very pretty and other things weren't quite what she would have liked. For instance, she had a nice smile, but her mouth was rather wide and her teeth had some awkward spaces between them. Lilibet wasn't very happy when the dentist had her start wearing rubber bands on her teeth, but she knew she would be glad later that she'd done it.

During the Coronation festivities the Princesses had gotten used to staying up quite late at night, so a part of "settling down" was getting back to their old bedtime. One warm July night they were put to bed early on the Royal Train, which was waiting in a London railway station. Later, when the King and Queen got aboard, the train would take the family to Scotland for summer vacation.

A railway policeman, walking the station platform to see that all was well, suddenly was surprised to hear a tapping sound coming from one of the train windows. He came nearer, alert for danger to the royal family. But what he saw through the open window was Princess Elizabeth in her nightgown, jumping up and down and tapping to attract his attention.

"Will you please go and get us a comic paper to read?" begged the little girl who had been so grand in coronet and robes in Westminster Abbey. "Please!" she added, holding out a shilling coin. The policeman wasn't sure just what he should do in a case like that. But he took the coin, walked off to the newsstand and brought the "comics" and the change to the Heiress Presumptive.

The Princesses loved also to read the magazines put out specially for children. They took quite a slice out of Lilibet's allowance, which was a shilling a week. She got the same amount from the time she was six years old until she was fourteen. Sometimes relatives gave her money as Christmas or birthday gifts. What she didn't spend she saved up for Christmas presents. Lilibet got quite a thrill when, at the age of thirteen, she checked up and found she had saved more than 30 pounds—about $125 in American money. She felt very rich.

* * *

Just like their parents, Elizabeth and Margaret were never happier than when they were in Scotland. That summer after the Coronation it seemed more wonderful than ever. Seven Scottish soldiers had been chosen to be the new King's official bagpipers. Every night, as dinner at Balmoral Castle was ending, they would march through the great hall and dining room in their bright plaid kilts to serenade the Royal Family with the sweet-sour music of the bagpipes.

On the broad, breezy moors the girls went picnicking with friends their own age and no grown-ups to get in the way. Some of the girls were "Girl Guides," the British name for Girl Scouts. Lilibet learned to fry potatoes and sausages when they "cooked out" on their picnics. By the time they went back to Buckingham Palace in the fall, the Princesses were full of the idea of joining the Girl Guides themselves. Miss Crawford suggested that they set up a Guide company at the Palace, for little girls whose fathers were court officials or employees.

So Lilibet, eager to learn how to tie knots and build a safe campfire, attended the first meeting she had ever called together. A dozen girls signed up. They called themselves the Kingfisher Patrol. Margaret, it turned out, was too young to be a Guide. This upset her terribly, but the girls solved the problem by organizing a Brownie Patrol called the Leprechauns.

The King's daughter would have dearly loved to be patrol leader of the Kingfishers. But in the Girl Guides this was something you got by earning it—not by being a Princess— and there were other Kingfishers who were older and more experienced. So, in her usual thorough way, Lilibet worked hard to pass her tests. The Buckingham Palace maids were surprised to find that they weren't allowed to make her bed these days. To earn one of her homemaking badges she had to learn to make it herself. And neatly, too. No lumps or wrinkles.

The maids weren't the only ones that were surprised. One Wednesday afternoon the Prime Minister, a rather humorless and proper man named Neville Chamberlain, came to the

In first aid drill Margaret gets bandaged while Elizabeth ties a sling.

Palace to confer with the King. When he looked out the window he was open-mouthed. Up and down the Palace lawn marched Princess Elizabeth with the Kingfishers, learning how to drill like one of her father's soldiers. Behind them trotted Margaret and the Leprechauns, a little less military but trying hard to keep up in spite of their short legs.

The two patrols held their meetings in a garden house that old King George V had used in the summer time. They rolled up the carpets when the weather was bad, and did their marching and turning indoors. Queen Elizabeth gave them a British flag and their own company flag of red and blue, and she attended the ceremony when they dedicated the new flags in the Palace chapel. Though the Princesses thought they were doing just what other girls were doing, you can see the Buckingham Palace company had rather fancier headquarters than most Girl Guides. To carry around their first aid equipment, signal flags and other gear, the King gave them a hand-cart painted navy blue with "Seventh Westminster Company" lettered in gold on the sides.

The King was especially pleased when, for their first Christmas, the Kingfishers and Leprechauns collected toys, clothes and candy to send to children in the London slums.

The King liked everything about the Girl Guides except the long black stockings that had always been part of the uniform. He said they were hideous and he wouldn't have his daughters wearing them. Probably the fathers of a lot of Girl Guides had thought the same thing, without being able to do anything about it. But when the Buckingham Palace Girl Guides blossomed out in beige socks that came to just below the knee, Guides all over England threw out their black stockings with a sigh of relief and switched to beige ones too.

It was as a Girl Guide that Lilibet made her first public appearance in uniform. This was in June, 1937, eight months after she joined. A thousand Guides from all over the British Empire paraded at Windsor Castle and held a service in St. George's Chapel. Though she had been christened there, the Heiress Presumptive to the throne wasn't allowed inside the chapel for the service. Only first-class Guides, those who had passed their advanced tests, were admitted. Not until she had been a Guide for two years, and earned a great many badges, did Lilibet become patrol leader of the Kingfishers.

❋ ❋ ❋

"Let's pretend!" For most of us, that wonderful game means pretending sometimes that we are Princesses. For Elizabeth and Margaret, it was just the other way around. They liked to pretend they were just like other girls, and studying homemaking and nature craft with the Guides and Leprechauns was all part of the game. It wasn't easy, though, to "rough it" in Buckingham Palace. A whole army of servants was always on hand to take care of the Royal Family, to give their parties for them, and to keep the big old building spic and span. Another army of secretaries and clerks worked in the Palace offices; they answered the thousands of letters the King received, and kept the records and the files. So many people worked for the Royal Family, in fact, that the Palace was more like a village than a residence. It had its own telephone system and its own postoffice and even a faithful postman who spent all day tramping around the corridors delivering letters.

The steward of the Palace, head of all the men servants, was the Princesses' old friend, Ainslie, who had been the family butler at 145 Piccadilly. Now he was in charge of the butlers and footmen, the pages who were there to run errands, the chefs in the kitchens and the porters who carried coal to hundreds of fireplaces. A woman, Mrs. Evans, was housekeeper for the Queen. Fifty housemaids in crisp uniforms got up while it was still dark to start their dusting and polishing and sweeping and bedmaking.

The Queen had a personal maid and two women called dressers to look after her clothes, and the King had two "valets"

75

to take care of his wardrobe. Besides Alla and Crawfie, each Princess had a personal maid—"Bobo" MacDonald for Lilibet and Bobo's sister, Ruby, for Margaret. The little girls even had a footman and a housemaid of their own, to take care of the nursery suite.

The Buckingham Palace footmen still wore the scarlet coats and white breeches that made them look like characters left over from the days when everyone danced the minuet. But they no longer wore powdered wigs—they just put some flour in their hair. Often the footmen were a great help, but sometimes Lilibet thought they were a nuisance. Especially when it came to dogs.

The Princesses had brought Dookie and Jane and Susan to the Palace with them, and Lilibet treasured the job of feeding them. But this wasn't as simple as it had been at 145 Piccadilly. Like so many things at the Palace, it had to be a regular ceremony. Every evening at 5 o'clock a red-coated footman marched solemnly up the corridor, with a checked cloth over his arm, carrying a bowl of food and a bowl of water. He put the cloth down on the hall carpet outside Lilibet's door, set the bowls on it, knocked and then went away. Lilibet would come out, with the dogs frisking at her heels, and stir up the food for them. Then she would stand by to see that they didn't eat too fast. When the dogs had had plenty of time to finish, the footman would reappear, pick up the dirty dishes and cloth, and disappear until the next night. So, you see, even the dogs had footmen at Buckingham Palace!

✻ ✻ ✻

As you can imagine, all this was pretty overwhelming for the little family from 145 Piccadilly; happily, everything was much the same as it had always been at Royal Lodge, where they still went for week-ends. The woodmen and the hired men in the stables and dog kennels didn't worry about saying "Princess" before they spoke to Lilibet or Margaret. They would even scold them—rather respectfully, of course—if they found the little girls doing something naughty or dangerous, like playing with a bonfire. There was plenty of horseback riding and lots of picnics in the Windsor groves. On these picnics Margaret loved to climb up on top of big tree stumps and yell out the rhyme from an old nursery game: "I'm the king of the castle! Get out, you dirty rascal!" She sounded very fierce and made faces to show how tough she was.

Lilibet practiced cooking in the Little House, and got so good she could bake and ice cakes to send to children in hospitals. Papa liked to work outdoors, so every Saturday afternoon the whole family put on old clothes and did some gardening. The King hacked and sawed away at dead tree limbs, the Queen went around snipping at shrubbery with pruning sheers, and the Princesses pulled weeds.

Lilibet and Margaret loved these week-ends because they had their father and mother more to themselves, like an ordinary family. Back in London, the King and Queen were so busy with official duties that their daughters were lucky to see them a couple of times a day. They still started the day with a morning visit, and there was usually time for a romp or a game of cards at teatime or before bed. But the King and Queen had to make lots of official appearances, and the King had a great deal of what we call "paper work" to do.

The British monarch has little real power these days, since the British people choose their government leaders by voting, just like Americans. But the King can advise these leaders, and

77

sometimes when there are disputes he tries to get the two sides together. And every evening a messenger arrives with black leather boxes full of official papers. These are bills passed by Parliament, and every one of them must be signed by the King before it becomes a law. Of course, he could just sign them without reading them, but George VI was a conscientious King—even though he couldn't veto laws as the President of the United States can do, he read everything carefully so he could understand just what was going on when government officials came for conferences.

Probably the King didn't work any harder than lots of fathers, but his daughters were learning that his job included a lot of tiresome duties. It mostly seemed to mean doing what other people wanted you to do, instead of what you wanted to do yourself. One of the Princesses' favorite poems summed it up exactly, even down to all the papers he had to sign. Probably you know the poem, too, since almost everyone has read what Mr. A. A. Milne had to say in *Buckingham Palace*:

> They're changing the guard at Buckingham Palace.
> Christopher Robin went down with Alice.
> They've great big parties inside the grounds,
> "I wouldn't be King for a hundred pounds,"
> > Says Alice.

> They're changing the guard at Buckingham Palace.
> Christopher Robin went down with Alice.
> A face looked out, but it wasn't the King's.
> "He's much too busy a-signing things,"
> > Says Alice.

There were other times when Lilibet and Margaret wouldn't have traded places with any other little girls in the world—even for a hundred pounds. For instance, who could ask for a better show, right in their own home, than the exciting nights when the King and Queen held court in the Palace Throne Room? To be presented at a Court is a great feather in one's cap for visitors from abroad, or for British girls making their debuts. Wearing their crowns and royal robes, the rulers sit on real thrones. These are big chairs upholstered in crimson with gold fringe and tassels and coats-of-arms embroidered on the back. The Throne Room has white walls and ceiling, with gold-trimmed carvings of angels and rosettes and leaves, like a fancy wedding cake. Crystal chandeliers shine down on the crimson carpet and draperies. The royal thrones are placed on a raised platform, under a crimson canopy, and above that is a balcony where an orchestra plays soft music.

To be presented, a person has to walk through that big room with everyone, including the King and Queen, watching. It makes everybody nervous—especially ladies. When a lady reaches the throne she must bend one knee in a low court curtsy—something she has been practicing frantically for weeks, to be sure of not toppling over.

On Court nights Lilibet and Margaret had a hard time eating much supper. They couldn't wait to go to the window to watch the big cars drive up. First the gentlemen stepped out, wearing the knee breeches required at Courts, and then came the ladies, with feather plumes in their hair and wearing evening dresses with trains five feet long. They were always most interested in the debutantes, the pretty young girls—not so many years older than Lilibet, really—who were having their first fling in grown-up society. Huddled at the window in their nightclothes Lilibet and Margaret told each other that some day, when they were old enough to be at a Court too, they would have the most beautiful gowns of anybody.

❋ ❋ ❋

Lilibet was "shooting up." She felt very tall and quite old compared with her little sister. For her twelfth birthday the Queen gave her her first pair of silk stockings. Papa had a special present: he let Lilibet be named president of the Children's League of the Princess Elizabeth of York Hospital for Children, one of the many hospitals named for her. In spite of these signs of growing up, Lilibet still ate most of her meals with Margaret in the nursery.

The Princesses ate simple meals—just about the same things that were favorites in most English homes. They had boiled beef or mutton, beef or rabbit stew, liver and bacon or steak-and-kidney pie. Like many other English children they were fond of steamed puddings and now and then they had ice cream as a special treat. Usually, though, the dessert was stewed fruit or gelatin or rice pudding. But this simple fare was served at the table by footmen in scarlet coats, and at every meal the menu was written out in French, to help the Princesses learn the language.

Except for the big dinner parties they gave on special occasions, the King and Queen also ate in much the same way as people living in less elegant homes. There was one big difference: the food was likely to be cold when it reached the royal couple! That was because the Palace kitchens were so far away from the royal apartments, and it was a problem to keep anything hot until it reached the table.

Another inconvenience of Palace life was the plumbing. Most of it was old-fashioned. The bathrooms had been added long after the Palace was built, and they were just parts of other rooms walled off with newer partitions. Some parts of the Palace had steam heat, but in most of the big rooms you got hot and pink-faced near the fireplace and nearly froze in the far corners.

One of the things the Princesses liked best at Buckingham Palace they had, you might say, earned themselves. About the time their father became King, Lilibet and Margaret started taking swimming lessons at the Bath Club in London. They loved it and worked hard at it—eager to be as good swimmers as the other girls they met at the pool. This pleased the King very much. He thought all children should learn to swim, both for fun and safety. He promised Lilibet and Margaret that if they made enough progress he would have a swimming pool built at the Palace. It took a couple of years, but when Lilibet had won the Bath Club swimming and lifesaving medals, Papa made good his promise. He had the Palace pool installed in a little glassed-in wing that had been a greenhouse. It was a little like swimming outside without ever leaving the building.

❊ ❊ ❊

Schoolwork with Miss Crawford went on six days a week, for Margaret as well as Lilibet. It seemed less and less likely, as the years passed, that the girls ever would have a little brother. So it was more and more likely that Elizabeth would someday be Queen. Most girls her age already are thinking about what they would like to be when they grow up. Lilibet wasn't free to choose her own career, but she was going to be a "career girl" just the same. And, even earlier than most girls,

The Dowager Queen Mary showed her grand-daughters
the sights of London. Here they are just leaving a museum.

she had to start learning the special things her job would require.

Miss Crawford saw to the formal studies; the King sponsored Lilibet in such health-building projects as her Guide work, swimming and riding, and Queen Mary turned out to be a great advocate of sight-seeing. She thought that—while books were important—nothing would teach the Princesses as much about the world outside the Palace as seeing for themselves. So every Monday afternoon, with their grandmother as "guide," they went out to look at something interesting. They visited the Tower of London and saw the Crown Jewels on display—the same jewels Mummie and Papa and Queen Mary had worn for the Coronation. At the British Museum they saw other crown jewels—the ones that had belonged to the ancient Egyptian kings, the Pharaohs they had read about in their history books. They went to the post office, to the Mint where British coins are made, to the Science museum, to Broadcasting House to see how a program called "The Children's Hour" was put on the air. At the London docks, their grandmother took them aboard a huge ocean liner that was named for Queen Mary herself.

No matter where the Princesses went, they usually felt very much like ordinary sightseers. This was because Queen Mary never allowed anybody to announce ahead of time where they were going. Often other visitors didn't even recognize Lilibet and Margaret, which was just what Queen Mary wanted. It was fine with the little girls, too.

But, of course, to the people who worked in the places the Princesses visited, they weren't ordinary sightseers at all. This was especially true of the London zoo, where the little girls went again and again. The zookeepers knew very well who they were, even when they arrived in a whole group of children. Lilibet and Margaret would run squealing from cage to cage, refusing guides because they knew just where they wanted to go, but greeting all the keepers like old friends. The keepers let them hold the baby animals—including a tiny alligator. Lilibet was allowed to feed a bear cub with condensed milk. Neither sister was afraid of snakes, and a keeper sometimes would stir up a cobra so they could see it coil and strike. They liked to tickle the puffer fish, which would promptly blow itself up like a balloon!

Lilibet considered herself quite an expert on the care and feeding of animals. One day she gave Margaret a good scolding for letting a couple of friendly elephants, Rani and Sally, have too many buns. Right in the middle of the lecture, Margaret broke into peals of laughter. As if to take Margaret's side and prove her big sister wrong, Rani had reached out her trunk and grabbed the whole sack of buns right out of Lilibet's hand.

* * *

In the spring of 1939 Lilibet and Margaret got a chance to prove they were "good soldiers" as well as royal princesses. Their father and mother packed up and left them for nearly two months. It was hard for Margaret to understand how she could be left behind, but Lilibet explained that it was part of royalty's job—the King and Queen had to make a Royal Tour of Canada, a member of the British Commonwealth of Nations. They also were going to pay a friendly but official visit to the United States.

When the little girls went down to the ship to see their parents off, they found they just couldn't say goodbye. The Princesses were still on board when it was past time for the big ship to sail, and the King had to tell them that they must go back to the dock. From there they waved and waved, with Margaret's little face all puckered up and Elizabeth bravely fighting back the tears that everyone could see in her eyes.

Once the sorrow of leave-taking was past, the Princesses buckled down hard to their lessons and wrote in their diaries every day so they would have something to show their parents when they got back. Lilibet and Margaret were taking the separation so well that Queen Mary and Miss Crawford decided they should be allowed to do something they especially wanted

28

The Princesses and Crawfie (third from right) meet a giant panda.

to do. And what do you think they had been begging for—for months? They wanted to ride on the London "underground"!

Thousands, even millions, of grown-ups and children ride on noisy subway trains twice a day and don't particularly like it. But for the Princesses it was just as exciting to do something ordinary children do as it would be for most people to live like royalty for a while.

So, one day, they arrived unannounced at a subway station with Miss Crawford and Lady Helen Graham, a lady-in-waiting to Queen Elizabeth. The little girls bought their tickets with money from their own purses, pushed through the turn-stiles, and waited on the platform for the right train to come along. With the rest of the crowd they surged into their train and then, wide-eyed, watched the other passengers, peered out the window and looked up at the subway map to see where they were. They changed trains once, taking an escalator to an-other level of the station. Lilibet made out all right but Marga-ret stepped on with the wrong foot and nearly lost her balance.

The Y.W.C.A., where they were going for tea, was almost as much of a novelty. The Princesses carried their own trays in the cafeteria, paid for their own tea and bread and butter, and drank the tea out of thick mugs—watching over the edge, while they gulped, to be sure of missing nothing.

Riding back on the subway a little trouble was added to the excitement. Margaret took charge of everybody's tickets, and she forgot to turn them in at the end of the trip. The ticket collector followed them into the street, waving his arms and demanding the stubs. Margaret begged his pardon with a smile, and then he recognized the Princesses—even if no one else had. He announced he was going to save their tickets as souvenirs.

Lilibet and Margaret were good letter writers and they wrote all about their subway expedition to Mummie and Papa. The Princesses were getting lots of mail, too. The King and Queen wrote long letters about their trip. They had seen Indians and cowboys in Canada. They had met the four-year-old Dionne Quintuplets—and one of the five little girls who looked alike had got so excited and confused that she gave her bouquet to the King instead of the Queen. They had seen Niagara Falls and New York, and had stayed with President and Mrs. Roosevelt in the White House. Papa wrote that he had been eating something wonderful called "hot dogs" in the United States!

One Sunday afternoon the Princesses had a real thrill. The King and Queen called them by radio-telephone from Ottawa, the capital of Canada, 3,000 miles away. When Margaret heard her parents' voices coming from clear across the Atlantic Ocean, she suddenly got shy and couldn't think of much to say. Lilibet tried to give the King and Queen all the news and answer all their questions before the 15-minute call was over.

When it was about time for the King and Queen's return, the maids gave the Palace a special housecleaning—and Lilibet and Margaret scrubbed and swept every inch of the Little House to have it ready for the homecoming. The day their parents were due, the Princesses had their first trip on a British Navy destroyer. It took them out into the middle of the English Channel to meet the Empress of Canada, the ship on which the King and Queen had crossed the Atlantic.

For a little bit it looked as if the seafaring British nation might have a couple of seasick princesses, but the girls quickly got over their strange feelings. There *were* a couple of shaky moments, though, when everybody—including Alla—had to jump from a ladder on the destroyer onto a bobbing little boat that was going to take them across to the Empress. They had to jump again from the little boat to a ladder put down by the big liner. But everybody made it, and a moment later Lilibet and Margaret were in their parents' arms.

After a lot of hugging and kissing, the Queen remarked to Miss Crawford that the Princesses looked very well and surely had grown. Lilibet, in fact, had grown so fast that she was really at what people called "the awkward age." But to her father she looked just wonderful. The ship's crew had hung colored balloons and streamers all over the place, and the King was so happy to be back with his daughters that he tossed balloons out the portholes so the girls could see them float away over the water.

When the family finally reached Buckingham Palace Lilibet and Margaret couldn't wait to start opening their presents. Hundreds of gifts had been sent to them from nearly every town the King and Queen had visited in Canada and the United States. There were dolls and Indian moccasins and hand-knitted sweaters and even some fierce-looking Indian totem poles. It took the King and Queen most of the summer to tell the little girls what they wanted to hear about the children overseas. The stories and presents made Lilibet feel she had a whole new world of friends in the countries she had studied about. But before the summer was over, something even bigger had happened to her—even though she didn't know it at the time.

❋ ❋ ❋

The King was going down to make an official inspection at Dartmouth Royal Naval College. This is something like the United States Naval Academy at Annapolis, except that the boys start a little younger. The King had gone to school there,

88

before he served in the Navy, and he wanted his daughters to see his old school. So the whole family, and Miss Crawford and Alla, too, sailed up the Dart River to Dartmouth on the Royal Yacht.

Suddenly, Lilibet and Margaret found themselves in the midst of 900 boys! Even one boy was always an object of curiosity to the Princesses, because they saw so few. Nine hundred of them, all in white uniforms and all studying to be naval officers, looked like all the boys in the world. The girls watched with fascination as the "cadets" marched and saluted and demonstrated that they already knew how to handle rowboats, motorboats and sailboats.

The teachers at Dartmouth are Navy officers, and the son and daughter of one of these officers had a toy train with lots of track. Lilibet was down on the floor playing with it when a tall, blond cadet came in and was introduced to her. He didn't seem especially impressed that she was a princess. He just knelt down beside her to play with the train, too.

It turned out that he was a prince—Prince Philip of Greece. But, just like Elizabeth herself, he was one of the many great-great-grandchildren of Queen Victoria of Great Britain. That made him a very distant cousin of Lilibet. He was a first cousin of Princess Marina of Greece, whom Lilibet and Margaret had admired so much ever since she married their youngest uncle, the Duke of Kent. Prince Philip had just turned eighteen years old and Lilibet, who was thirteen, thought he was terribly good-looking.

The Heiress Presumptive couldn't stop looking at Philip, Miss Crawford noticed, and the next day when he came to tea aboard the Royal Yacht she made just as much fuss over him. She kept asking him what he would like to eat and passing him one dish after another. Lilibet blushed quite a lot but she knew enough just to be nice and friendly without really overdoing it, so they got along very well indeed. Philip teased Margaret about being plump. Margaret, it was true, thought eating was a very fine pastime. So when Philip polished off several plates of shrimp and topped them off with a banana split, she was just as goggle-eyed with admiration as Lilibet.

The royal family sailed away the next day, and the Dartmouth cadets followed the yacht out to sea in their little boats. The King worried for fear the boys were getting too far from shore and signaled them to go back. They all did—except Philip, who kept right on rowing behind the yacht. Lilibet watched him through a pair of field glasses but the King did not think much of this performance. Philip finally got the idea that the King wasn't happy about him, and he disappeared in the distance. Lilibet put the field glasses away. But she would never feel quite like a little girl again.

CHAPTER SIX

A Princess in Uniform

This is how a career princess helps her country win a war.

IT WAS AN UNEASY SUMMER, that year of 1939. Lilibet was reading the London newspapers every day, as part of her school work, so she was very much "up" on the news. She knew that Hitler, the man with the little black mustache, already had sent the German army into Austria and Czechoslovakia. She knew that her father's Prime Minister, Mr. Chamberlain, the man with the big black umbrella, was trying to stop Hitler without getting so tough that Britain would have to fight Germany. The year before Mr. Chamberlain had given in to some of Hitler's demands, saying this would guarantee Britain "peace in our time." Like many of her countrymen, Lilibet was beginning to wonder if this were true.

Everybody was so upset that the King and Queen and the Princesses weren't even sure they could go up to Scotland that summer. It was August 7 before the King finally decided to make the trip. Lilibet and Margaret would never have believed it, if anyone had told them how long it would be before they saw London again.

They were happy once more in their beloved Scotland, until the news came in on September 1 that Hitler had attacked Poland. At first Lilibet couldn't understand why this upset her father so, but before long she knew. On September 3, Prime Minister Chamberlain declared war on Germany! Papa explained that Britain and France had promised in a treaty to come to Poland's aid if anyone ever attacked that small country. Within a few days the British Dominions of Canada, Australia, New Zealand and South Africa had declared war, too.

Lilibet felt both sad and alarmed that peace had ended for her country. She had studied about a great many wars, and she knew danger lay ahead.

Because of the English Channel, the Germans couldn't just march into England. But nobody knew when they might send their war planes over to drop bombs on it. London, of course, would be a choice target. In spite of this danger, the King and Queen hurried back to the city. But like thousands of other British parents, they wanted to safeguard their children. So Lilibet and Margaret stayed on in Scotland, moving

At "school" at Windsor in 1940, the Princesses paint and sketch.

over to friendly little Birkhall on the Balmoral Castle grounds. Miss Crawford broke off her own vacation to come and join them.

* * *

Almost overnight, it seemed, the whole nation looked like a different country. Half the people suddenly were in uniform, of one kind or another. In every home and factory the lighted windows were "blacked out" with dark, heavy material. This was so the lights would not show the German bombing planes where the cities were.

Lilibet and Margaret worried a lot about their parents. They knew London was in more danger than Scotland, and Margaret simply couldn't understand why Papa and Mummie had to be there. The King and Queen found the separation pretty painful, but in one way it was a help. When the Queen urged other mothers to send their children to the country, away from the bombs, she could say: "I know myself how sad it is to be apart from the children. But it is best for them."

Just before Christmas the royal parents decided it wasn't necessary to be so *far* apart. They moved the Princesses down to Windsor Castle, which was far enough from London to be fairly safe but close enough so they could all be together on weekends.

The whole trip was a great big secret. Nobody wanted the Germans to find out, for fear they might bomb the Castle. Many people thought the Princesses were still in Scotland. Others heard rumors that the girls had been sent to Canada, where many British children went for safety's sake. The Germans heard this story and believed it. They even broadcast it as news, and said it was a sure sign that Britain knew she was going to lose the war. In a few months, as we shall see later, the Princesses made that claim look foolish.

For the time being, though, it was a good thing the girls' whereabout was kept quiet. It was no secret that the King and Queen were staying on in London—they had to set an example of bravery. As a result, the Germans bombed Buckingham Palace nine times before the war was over. The King and Queen were never hurt, but more than once the explosions blew state papers right out of the King's hand. One bomb made a direct hit on the Princesses' swimming pool!

Lilibet and Margaret had stayed at Windsor Castle many times, but they had never really lived there before. It was much safer than Royal Lodge, their own home a mile-and-one-half away in Windsor Great Park. The Castle had been built as a fortress, with sturdy, thick stone walls and towers. Its underground dungeons, where ancient kings had kept their prisoners, made a natural air raid shelter.

All over England, in those days, people raced for the shelters when the air raid sirens sounded the alarm that German bombers were coming. Lilibet and Margaret were supposed to go right down to the dungeons when the alarm went off, even if it was in the middle of the night. Since Alla wouldn't let them just put coats over their nightgowns, the Princesses each got a "siren suit." This was a sort of a coverall that you could zip into in a hurry.

The little girls found the dark old dungeons rather scary, with shadows flitting in the dim light, but they were quite brave about the air raids. While planes droned overhead, Lilibet and Margaret calmly drank tea and wrote in their diaries. Later, when the bombing was at its worst, they went to the dungeons every evening at 7 o'clock and stayed all night. By that time a bedroom and bathroom had been fixed up for them, and there was another for the King and Queen to use when they came to Windsor on week-ends.

Lilibet was much interested in the war, and she wanted to do everything she could to help win it. One day she heard that old scrap iron could be melted down and used again. She promptly enlisted Margaret, and the two Princesses walked all over the Windsor acres with a garden cart, searching for old nails and pots and hinges. That week-end, when Papa saw the pile they had collected, he thought it was pretty funny. Some of the things were so rusty the King didn't think they could ever be any good for *anything* again. But to show the Princesses he appreciated their effort, Papa put a few pieces of old iron on the pile himself.

Gardening was something else the girls could do for the war effort. All over Britain children were planting vegetable gardens. So the Princesses turned their own little plots at Windsor into "Victory gardens," and grew all sorts of vegetables. This was important, because the German submarines were trying to starve Britain by sinking the ships that usually brought in food. When plums in the royal orchard were falling from the trees for lack of pickers, the Princesses picked them for a jam factory. And when the government asked people to give aluminum to help make airplanes, Lilibet turned in tiny pots and pans from her own Little House!

Lilibet kept maps with colored pins to show how the war was going on each battle front, and she rarely missed a broadcast of war news. She was learning to recognize all kinds of airplanes and she studied everything she could find about the ships of the British Navy. Her trip aboard a destroyer had made her feel very close to the Navy—and knowing that handsome Navy cadet, Prince Philip, helped, too.

❊ ❊ ❊

In May of 1940 a terrible thing happened. Hitler's armies drove through Holland and Belgium into France, and cornered a British army of 350,000 men. The government rounded up just about everything that would float, from warships to tiny fishing boats, and sent them across the channel to rescue these men. Most of them were taken off the beaches of the little French town of Dunkerque—a name that became famous in the war. The success of this daring stroke, right under Hitler's nose, made the British almost as happy as if they had won a victory.

But now there was a great deal of talk about a German invasion of England. The "blitz," as the German air attack on Britain was called, grew fiercer every night. As many as a thousand bombing planes would come across the Channel in the night to drop hundreds of tons of bombs on London, and even some on the town of Windsor. Some countries might have quit under this kind of attack—but something wonderful as well as something awful had happened. The King had a new Prime Minister to replace Mr. Chamberlain. He was a blunt, stocky man who looked just like the cartoons of "John Bull," and he was just as stubborn and determined. His name was Winston Churchilll.

With the Germans lined up on the coast of France, only twenty or thirty miles across the channel from England, the new Prime Minister made a speech that thrilled Britain and the whole world. In it he said:

". . . we shall defend our Island, whatever the cost may be, we shall fight on the beaches, we shall fight on the landing grounds, we shall fight in the fields and in the streets; we shall fight in the hills; we shall never surrender . . ."

These words lit a fire in every British heart—including Lilibet's. Behind such a man the loyal people of England, Scotland and Wales were ready for anything. And in the long, terrible summer of 1940 they won "The Battle of Britain." The brave young men of the Royal Air Force drove the Germans right out of the skies, and by fall the tide had begun to turn. The

With Margaret looking on, Elizabeth makes her first broadcast.

Princesses felt grateful that history had provided a Winston Churchill to inspire the nation.

❊ ❊ ❊

After listening to Mr. Churchill's wonderful speeches, Lilibet felt rather humble when she was asked to speak to the nation. The King and the government decided in October, 1940, that it was time to let the Germans know the Princesses were still around. Lilibet was just halfway between fourteen and fifteen years old, and it was the first time she had ever talked to a large audience.

Her speech was only three minutes long, but she rehearsed it carefully, learning to stay exactly the right distance from the microphone. The Princess's message was mainly for British children, especially those who had been sent to safety overseas. Millions of people all over the world, grown-ups as well as children, heard Lilibet's clear, high voice as she said:

"I can truthfully say to you all that we children at home are full of cheerfulness and courage. We are trying to do all we can to help our gallant soldiers, sailors and airmen, and we are trying, too, to bear our share of the danger and sadness of war. We know, every one of us, that in the end all will be well, for God will care for us and give us victory and peace."

As usual, Lilibet was anxious not to have Margaret left out. So just before the broadcast ended, the audience heard her tell her ten-year-old sister: "Say good-night, Margaret." And Margaret piped up, "Good night, children!" Lilibet was being especially motherly to the younger girl, now that the Queen was away from them so much of the time. She didn't think people ought to talk about "battles and things" when Margaret was around. "We don't want to upset her," she told Miss Crawford.

❊ ❊ ❊

One thing Lilibet and Margaret both liked about the way people were living in wartime: it gave them a whole new set of friends. Lots of children from London had come to stay with families who lived and worked on the huge royal estate at Windsor. Many were from the poorer sections of the city— children the Princesses never would have met while they were living at Buckingham Palace.

At Windsor they all belonged to the same Girl Guide troop and got to know each other very well. On summer nights, after the "blitz" was over, they slept outdoors together, each

99

snuggling down in her own "flea bag," or sleeping bag. Lilibet worked especially hard at earning her merit badges for cooking. She and a dozen other Guides met in the housekeeper's kitchen at the castle and learned to make cakes and pies and biscuits and soups and stews.

A cake was a big event. People in England got very small amounts of scarce foods, like eggs and sugar and even milk. They were "rationed" to make them go around fairly. For a long time Lilibet and Margaret got just one egg a week. Usually they had it for Sunday morning breakfast, but when the Guides wanted to bake a cake they all had to save their egg rations and put them together. Then they would have a tea party and share the cake with some of the young officers who were on duty at Windsor to protect the castle.

The officers would come to weekly movies at the castle, too, and sometimes the Princesses would invite them to lunch. There were a lot of American soldiers in the neighborhood, too. They often had candy when the British didn't, and would delight the Princesses with a real treat—a box of chocolates. The older American officers would pull out snapshots of their own children to show the girls. So many of them said, "I have a little girl back home just your age," that the Princesses could hardly keep from laughing. Margaret finally told Miss Crawford there must be "simply billions" of children in America, "all our age."

✳ ✳ ✳

Lilibet and Margaret still did their lessons with Miss Crawford, but Lilibet had another tutor now, too. He was Sir Henry Marten, and he was assistant to the headmaster of Eton College, the famous old English school for boys. Eton is just across a bend in the Thames River from Windsor Castle.

At first Lilibet went twice a week to Eton, where the boys tipped their hats politely to the future Queen—even though some of them looked as if they would rather wink instead. Lilibet thought their uniforms were wonderful. The hats they tipped were high silk toppers. They wore striped dark trousers, white bow ties, and the short coats that are known everywhere as Eton jackets.

The main thing that Lilibet studied with Sir Henry was British constitutional history. This meant that she learned what part the monarchy had played in her country's life, and what role the monarch still had to perform. She also learned more about United States history than any previous heir to the throne. The gentle, bald-headed Sir Henry was pleased when he found that Lilibet was curious about nearly everything. When she asked why Windsor Great Park had to be plowed up and planted to crops, he gave her a course in British agriculture. She learned a lot about the food problems of the nation, and the special problems of farmers.

Lilibet became quite fond of this elderly man, who had so many books and knew what was in them all. She discovered he liked sweet things as well as any child did. They were hard to get in England during the war, but people were always sending Lilibet presents from America and other countries. So every week she gave Sir Henry two pounds of honey. It was a little way of showing that she knew he was helping her do a better job at the career that was all picked out for her.

One Sunday, not long before Lilibet was sixteen, there was a pretty little service in the Windsor Castle Chapel to mark her confirmation in the Church of England. The King and Queen and Queen Mary were there to see the ceremony. Lilibet wore a white dress and carried a white prayer book with "E" on the back of it. The service made her feel very serious, and made her think of all that lay ahead for her in the future.

✳ ✳ ✳

Anybody's sixteenth birthday is a big milestone. But it's a rare girl who can expect, on that day, to become the colonel of her own regiment of dashing Guardsmen! That was what happened to Lilibet. She became the first woman colonel the Grenadier Guards (the First, or Senior, regiment of the five that make up the Brigade of Guards) had ever had. It was the King who appointed her, and he seemed to be telling the British Commonwealth that its "little Princess" was growing up and was about to take on the public duties of royalty. For her first official post the King couldn't have picked anything more exciting to a girl who had always loved military music and parades and uniforms.

The Guards with their scarlet uniforms and bearskin hats play colorful roles in peacetime ceremonies, but they also are great fighters. The Grenadiers already had fought the Germans in France, and they were just waiting to be sent into battle again. On that April 21, 1942, they marched in review for Lilibet at Windsor Castle, each man saluting her as his senior officer by turning his head—as stiffly as a tin soldier—as he passed the Princess.

More like a woman than a colonel, Lilibet had thought quite a bit about what she would wear that day. Clothes, like food, were rationed in wartime, and clothes of "utility" quality were easier to get. So Princess Elizabeth made her first big public appearance in a double-breasted, blue-green "utility" suit cut on simple lines. She added, however, a touch of her own. The hat she chose was of blue-green felt, shaped like a beret, but with the top jutting forward like the sun visor on a military cap. On it she wore the insignia of the Grenadiers—a gold badge in the shape of a flaming grenade.

The Guardsmen were delighted with their Princess-colonel. As a birthday present they gave her another grenadier's badge, only this one was made up of diamonds. Lilibet said a little thank-you speech that she made up as she went along. And the hat was a hit all over England. As soon as "Colonel Lilibet's" picture appeared in the papers, "Princess hats" became best-sellers.

That evening Lilibet and the King and Queen paid a surprise visit to the Sergeants' Mess of the Grenadiers. When a

The Grenadier Guards salute Elizabeth on her sixteenth birthday.

sixteen-year-old drummer boy boldly asked her to dance the Princess accepted. They had a fine, lively foxtrot.

* * *

Under a wartime law, every Briton over sixteen years old had to register for "national service." If they didn't volunteer for the armed forces or a war job, the government could assign them where they were needed most. Some wealthy and rather snobbish parents thought signing up at a "labor exchange" was beneath their daughters' position in life. They didn't have much argument left when the King's daughter did it.

A few days after her birthday Lilibet put on her Girl Guide uniform and went down to the branch office of the Ministry of Labor in the town of Windsor. She walked up to the wooden counter and told the two girl clerks all the things they needed to know to fill out her registration card. Then, like everyone else who registered, she was given a number. To the Ministry of Labor she became simply Briton No. SWGC 55-1.

It was up to the King and his Cabinet to decide whether the Princess should actually go into some kind of wartime "national service." They decided not. Nothing, they announced, should interrupt her training for queenship—her own kind of "national service." Lilibet, who always wanted to do what other girls were doing, was disappointed. But by now she knew herself that she had a big job to get ready for. Every week-end her father would open the dispatch boxes and go through the state papers with the Princess, explaining the various bills and what a King (or Queen) had to do about them. Lilibet also worked hard on her studies, and now that she was old enough she got into an exciting new branch of the Girl Guides.

Father and daughter study the "home work" of a king – or queen.

With Miss Crawford's help, she organized a troop of Sea Rangers. They are like Sea Scouts, only for girls. To be a Sea Ranger, you have to be an outstanding Girl Guide, with a great many merit badges. The girls around Windsor who made the grade included a typist, an office clerk, a nursemaid and the daughter of one of the grooms in the royal stables. Princess Elizabeth wasn't the captain of her "ship," as the Sea Rangers call their troops. But she soon was promoted to be "bos'n of the starboard watch."

The Sea Rangers weren't just dry-land sailors, either. Papa gave them a life boat and some rowboats, and they had the use of a motor launch. So they got plenty of real practice on the nearby Thames River and the lake in Windsor Great Park. In the winter and on rainy days, they practiced seamanship in—of all places!—the Waterloo Room of Windsor Castle. This room was named for the great land victory Britain won over Napoleon. With the King's permission, a complete copy of the "bridge" of a warship was built there. The "bridge" is where the captain and his assistants steer the vessel, give orders and keep watch. The "Duke of York," as the Rangers named their "ship" in thanks to the King, had a compass, a "helm" or steering wheel, speaking tubes, maps and charts, a telegraph set, Navy signal flags, and lifebelts for the whole "crew." Bos'n Lilibet could pace its deck and imagine she was doing some of the same things a real Navy man would be doing. Especially a Navy man named Prince Philip.

❋ ❋ ❋

As the long war went on and kept them at Windsor, the Princesses had to make most of their own fun. Both girls had always enjoyed going to the theater. They were particularly fond of the fairy-tale plays called "pantomimes" that are put on for British children during the Christmas season. What could be more fun, they decided one day, than staging a pantomime themselves? Almost before anybody could say yes or no, the Princess had everybody at Windsor organized into her stage company.

"Cinderella" was their first pantomime. The master of the Royal School at Windsor wrote the playlet—with plenty of advice from the Princesses. They rang in all the royal family jokes they could think of. Lilibet, who would have got no thrill out of playing a Princess, played a Prince. She was Prince Charming. She wore a satin coat and knee breeches, and a powdered wig. Margaret was Cinderella. She had a powdered wig, too, and a beautiful ruffled crinoline gown to wear when she rode to the ball in her coach.

The pantomime was a great success, so they gave three more of them. Everybody sold tickets and altogether the Princesses and their supporting cast (mostly children from the Royal School) made $3,000. The money went to the Queen's Wool Fund, which was used to buy yarn for volunteer knitters. Lilibet had made such a charming Prince Charming that the next year she played a prince again in "Sleeping Beauty" and the year after that she was Aladdin. But by 1944, when Lilibet was eighteen, her father decided it was time she played different parts. So this time she played the role of Lady Christina Sherwood.

For this fourth pantomime the Princesses mixed all the old nursery rhymes together and called their show "Old Mother Red Riding Boots." It was a regular variety show. The Princesses and the rest of the cast sang and danced to popular tunes of the day, like "It's Foolish But It's Fun," "Swinging on a Star," and "In My Arms."

For their big duet together, Lilibet and Margaret sang the old French nursery rhyme, "Sur le Pont d'Avignon." They did it sweetly and soberly, the way it was written. Then, with mischief in their eyes, they suddenly broke into "swing time" and sang it again as they did a jaunty tap dance that nearly brought down the house. The King and Queen were in the front row, and they had hardly recovered from this when Margaret reappeared to sing "Come Into the Garden, Maud." This was written by the dignified British poet, Lord Tennyson, but Margaret sang it with a broad Cockney accent—and the King laughed until he had to wipe tears from his eyes.

Margaret got so worked up about the pantomime that by the time the day came she was, as Miss Crawford said, "pea green" and sick in bed. But she always bounded out in time to go on stage and make a hit. Lilibet took her stage "career" quite calmly—except for one year. That was 1943, when they were doing "Aladdin." As she made her entrance by popping out of a laundry basket, she glanced nervously at the front row. There, with the King and Queen, sat Prince Philip. Although Lilibet knew he was going to attend, she still had a wave of stage-fright. Philip was on a Christmas leave from the Navy, and the Queen had invited him to spend the holiday at Windsor.

At twenty-two Philip was a tall, lean, well-mannered Navy officer, not very much like the brash boy Lilibet had first met four years before. His eyes were the same bright, deep blue, but the war had given them a serious expression. The Prince was a gay companion for the holidays, though, and he made every night a party while he was at the castle. By the time he went back to his ship he and Lilibet had promised to write to each other.

❋ ❋ ❋

After Lilibet was eighteen (in 1944), she began to make more public appearances and take on more official duties. At

In Christmas pantomime "Aladdin" Elizabeth played the title role.

the King's request Parliament passed a law making Princess Elizabeth one of the five Councillors of State. Their job was to act in place of the King if he should be ill or out of the country. Her father decided, too, that she should make her first official public tour. She went with the King to Wales to visit war factories, mines and dockyards.

If Lilibet had reached eighteen in normal times, she might have looked forward to a gay year of fashionable State balls, theater and dinner parties, and horseshow and opera visits. Instead of the soft light of candles and crystal chandeliers, the glare of a Welsh blast furnace shone on her "debut." In place of soft background music, the roar of machinery drowned out her words and all but swallowed up the cheers of sweating, grimy metal workers. The Welsh people, who long ago had sent her the Little House, still thought of Lilibet as "Ein Twysoges" – "Our Princess." They knew that, if she had been a boy, she would have been Prince of Wales, and they had always hoped that her father would give her the title of Princess of Wales.

This late spring of 1944 was a time of great tension and excitement in England. Britain and the United States and their Allies were planning to invade the European continent. Lilibet and her parents visited many secret training centers. They watched the final "battle practice" of tank battalions and the "dress rehearsal" jumps of parachute troops. At one American air station she christened a U.S. bomber named "Rose of York" in her honor. When the great invasion began on June 6, Lilibet stayed glued to her radio. She only wished that she could have gone along.

Now that the big offensive to win the war was actually underway, Lilibet was more eager than ever to have a part in the struggle. She had tried hard to accept the decision of King George and the Cabinet. But even a King's daughter could coax her father—and, in this case, change a Cabinet's mind. A month before her nineteenth birthday an announcement came from Buckingham Palace. It told a great deal about the "left out" feelings a Princess could have. Princess Elizabeth, the announcement said, had joined the ATS—the Auxiliary Territorial Service. This was like the American WAC, or women's branch of the army. The King had given her the lowest possible officers' rank: second subaltern. She was going to learn how to drive and take care of army cars, trucks and ambulances.

So Princess Elizabeth, the Colonel of the Grenadier Guards, put on greasy coveralls and broke her fingernails learning to change tires and wheels. With other ATS girls in training, she practiced taking gasoline engines apart and putting them together again. She got her hands grimy and her face streaked as she learned to grind valves and adjust carburetors.

At first her ATS comrades stared at Lilibet curiously. A Princess in khaki uniform or work coveralls was, after all, quite a sight. One girl driver caught a glimpse of Lilibet and took her eyes off the road. She crashed her car into a post and knocked it sideways. The leaning post was left that way, to remind others to keep their minds on their jobs. Before long Lilibet was making friends with the other trainees. Although she went home to Windsor Castle every night, she ate her meals in the ATS officers' mess. And her rank was so low that she had to salute most of the other officers. (She eventually got a promotion.)

Lilibet's great moment of triumph came one day when she drove from the training center into London. No one recognized her. As she threaded her way through the tangled

London traffic, she got all the whistles and shouts of advice that male drivers—especially soldiers—always offered to girls in khaki driving army cars. Lilibet sped into the red gravel driveway of Buckingham Palace just at dinner time, when her parents' guests were arriving in sleek black cars with chauffeurs. She'll probably never forget the look on the gatekeeper's face!

One day word reached the training center that King George, Queen Elizabeth and Princess Margaret were coming to make an inspection. This threw everybody into a frenzy of cleaning quarters, pressing uniforms, and shining brass buttons. When the royal visitors arrived Elizabeth was not to be seen. Finally, as they moved from one workshop to another, Margaret spotted her sister. With a group of girls, Lilibet was working on a truck engine. She was half inside it, but she crawled out, looking hot and smudged. Margaret, who had been dying to be in uniform herself, decided maybe the whole thing wasn't so glamorous after all. At last Lilibet knew what it was like to be on "the other end" of a royal inspection.

❊ ❊ ❊

By the time Lilibet's training was over, the war in Europe was over, too. It happened so suddenly that no one could quite believe it. May 8, 1945, was V-E Day, or Victory-in-Europe Day, for the Allies. The Germans had surrendered and London, like New York and every other Allied city or country town, was in a fever of joy and relief.

Crowds surged toward Buckingham Palace and with cheers and shouts urged the King and Queen to come out on the balcony. They appeared, waving and smiling, and bringing with them the great wartime Prime Minister, Winston Churchill, to take the bow he so justly deserved for the victory. With them, too, were Lilibet and Margaret—Lilibet in her ATS uniform, taking movies with the camera she had got so expert with. It was a great moment. But nobody in the Palace, or out of it, forgot that Britain was still at war. The Germans' allies, the Japanese, were still fighting in the far-away Pacific. And British airmen and sailors were still risking their lives there to make the victory complete. The real Victory Day came about three months later, when the Japanese surrendered too.

Once again the Royal Family came out on the balcony to answer the roaring crowds. But as the evening wore on and the celebration grew more and more exciting, the Princesses decided they wanted to really be *in* it. Papa thought it would be all right, if a couple of Guards officers went along. So Lilibet and Margaret, both in ordinary clothes, slipped out the gate and into the crowd. They joined in the calls for the King and Queen and Lilibet, like a lot of other people, took snapshots of everything. With the crowd, the Princesses sang "God Save the King" and "Auld Lang Syne." They had seldom had so much fun!

On the happiest day of her life Princess Elizabeth and Philip respond to London's salute as they leave Westminster Abbey.

CHAPTER SEVEN

Elizabeth the Bride

THE CURTAIN WAS ABOUT TO GO UP on the first act of *While the Sun Shines,* a comedy hit of the London theater season. It was November 12, 1945, and the British were enjoying the cheerful new mood that followed six years of war. As the chattering theater-goers found their seats, a party of seven young people arrived. One look at the group sent the doorman and ushers buzzing into action. The manager hurried up, mopping his brow and worrying for fear there had been some mistake. No one had told him to expect guests in the royal box that evening.

The royal box wasn't wanted. Princess Elizabeth had come to the theater with four young Guards officers, her young lady-in-waiting, the Honorable Mrs. Vicary Gibbs, and fifteen-year-old Princess Margaret. It was the first time the Princesses had ever gone out publicly in the evening without older members of the royal family. But Elizabeth had decided long ago that the royal box was no place to sit to watch a play. You had to look at everything from a one-sided angle. So one of the Guards officers had quietly reserved their tickets for the fourth row of the regular seats.

The evening was a great success, and before the winter was over Londoners got used to seeing the Princess in carefully-chosen public places with girls and young men of her own age. For Elizabeth, after years of quiet upbringing, was being allowed to have a bit of a "fling." A few weeks after the theater party she went to dinner with friends at a restaurant called the Bagatelle. She wore a shoulder corsage on her sheer black dress—perhaps to celebrate her first public "dining out" since she and Margaret took the subway to the Y.W.C.A.

The end of the war gave Lilibet a chance to renew an old interest in horse-racing. She was still in ATS uniform when she went to the big horse-racing meet at Ascot. Women are almost never allowed in the jockey's weighing room at any race track, but the Ascot officials invited Elizabeth to watch the riders step on the scales. The wiry little men trooped in, wearing their bright silk riding uniforms and carrying their saddles under their arms. The Princess saw the surprise and disbelief in their faces as they glimpsed a girl in khaki. She gave them back an amused, friendly smile.

The riders would have been more surprised to find how easily Lilibet could have talked with them about horse breeding and track records. Or to learn that she had gone alone to the Newmarket track, at 6 o'clock on a chill morning, to time the royal family's own racers. Lilibet's interest in the royal racing stable reminded many Britons of her fun-loving great-grandfather, King Edward VII. And when she was thrown by her horse that summer and got right back on again, it reminded others of her Uncle David, Edward VIII, who was now the Duke of Windsor. Many people still had a soft spot in their hearts for the Duke, though the royal family rarely spoke of him and had never received his wife, the Duchess.

* * *

British society did its best to stage a comeback that first winter after the war, in spite of the new Labor Party government that had been elected to succeed Winston Churchill's Conservative Party. The Labor Party hoped to do away with great differences in income and leisure and privilege. That plan made some members of society pretty unhappy, but it didn't bother the Princesses very much. Like the rest of the royal family, they were supposed to take an interest in politics but never to express an opinion about them.

But what nineteen-year-old girl would not be glad that her first postwar winter offered supper dances and dinner parties and balls? Lilibet loved to dance, and she was as good at fox trots, tangos, rhumbas and romantic waltzes as she was at Highland reels. At private dances the Princess liked to lead a conga line. Sometimes at Buckingham Palace or Windsor Castle the long, swaying line of dancers would follow her down the red-carpeted corridors and through the gilt-and-plush state apartments. She always had her favorites among the hit tunes of the day. But there were some that were her "all-time" favorites, like "Night and Day," "Let's Fall in Love," and the swingy, modern version of "Sur le Pont d'Avignon."

One night, when it came time for the band to go home, Lilibet just couldn't bear to have the dancing stop. Her cousin, Captain the Honorable Andrew Elphinstone, was at the party too and he was a good pianist. So Lilibet coaxed him into playing for nearly an hour more.

Many of the balls and theater engagements were "benefits," held to raise money for some worthy cause. The King and Queen, in brilliant formal dress, would attend to show their support of the project. Often, at such times, famous stars of the movies or theater were presented to the royal family. For Lilibet these appearances, like private parties, called for her prettiest long, pastel evening dresses, long white gloves, and her white fur evening wrap.

Nearly always there were young, titled gentlemen or officers in the royal party, and as the year went on the British people busily played the game of match-making. All the young men called Elizabeth "Ma'am," in the proper way, unless she knew them very well indeed and asked them to call her "Princess." But you would have thought, from all the talk and newspaper gossip, that every time Elizabeth's picture was taken with a new escort she was just about to marry him.

While everybody was asking the question "Who?", the answer was on a desk in Buckingham Palace, in a suite that now was Lilibet's own. Only not many people had a chance to see this clue—and if they had, they might not have recognized it. It was a picture of Prince Philip. But Lilibet wanted to keep her secret. So the picture she had on display was of Philip with the full, blond beard he had grown while his ship was at sea during the war. She didn't think anybody could see through all those whiskers!

Elizabeth and Philip had written to each other faithfully ever since that Christmas, two years earlier, when he had stayed at Windsor Castle. He had made a fine record in the Navy. At Dartmouth Naval College he won the prize as the best all-around cadet, and at twenty-one he became the First Lieutenant of the destroyer *Whelp*. He was the youngest officer in the Navy to hold such a position. He served in the Mediterranean Sea and the Atlantic Ocean.

One day in 1946 the peacetime world suddenly seemed much brighter to Lilibet, who had really been dancing with only half a heart. Philip was back in England! He was going to be an instructor at a Navy training center. He soon began to show up at the same parties where Princess Elizabeth was invited.

There still were other young men who escorted her just as often—or oftener. That was all right with Lilibet. She and Philip had to be very careful. This was one romance she didn't want to be common gossip until she—and he—were ready to talk about it. They danced together very rarely, but they could look at each other as they passed with other partners. They saw the American musical show, *Oklahoma!*, and felt as if its lovely ballad, "People Will Say We're in Love," was truly "our song." Lilibet played it over and over on her phonograph. When she and Philip dined and danced at restaurants with friends, she would quietly ask the band to play the tune.

* * *

Meanwhile, life was not all dancing for Elizabeth, who knew as well as anyone that you must also "work to pay the violins." She was taking over a greater share of the royal family's public appearances. During 1945 she had made thirty, but in 1946 she made that many in the first five months. Sometimes they came at a rate of four a week. She had to make a lot of speeches, too, though somebody else wrote the long ones for her. She was right in the middle of one, one day, trying to hang on to her hat and her skirt in a high wind, when her notes blew out of her hand. Everybody else was more alarmed than Elizabeth. She had studied her subject, so she went right ahead and made up the rest of the speech out of her own head.

Miss Crawford was one of the many people who deeply admired Elizabeth's strong sense of duty. Even when she was feeling ill—which was rare—or tired, she would brush off any suggestions that she should cancel a public appearance. "I've just got to do it," she would say, "after all, it's my job." More and more people remarked, these days, that the Princess resembled Queen Mary as a young woman. They thought that she had the same sense of duty, too, but then her own father and mother had also worked hard at their jobs.

Often Lilibet was almost the only young person present in a dignified gathering of gray-haired gentlemen and dowagers. Whenever she could, though, she gave her special attention to youth welfare groups like the Girl Guides, children's hospitals and training schools. She was the honorary president of the Royal College of Music and of the Royal Orchestral Society. She gave her time to many musical events—including the first concert of the National Federation of Jazz Organizations. Though Lilibet no longer had schoolwork to do, she kept up her own music and her French at home. Miss Crawford revived the madrigal classes she had started at Windsor during the war, and the Princesses would ask 30 or 40 young people to sing together in the Bow Room of the Palace. Afterward, they would have sherry and sweet biscuits.

By now, you can see, Elizabeth was a sort of "career princess." The family realized that she had to begin making a life of her own. She had her own "apartment" of bedroom and sitting room at the Palace, and her own staff of employes. Besides "Bobo" MacDonald, her personal maid, there was a housemaid and a footman. Old Alla had died just after the war, and Miss Crawford spent most of her time with Margaret now. Elizabeth had one lady-in-waiting and she was about to add another because she had so many letters to answer, engagements to keep track of and requests for help.

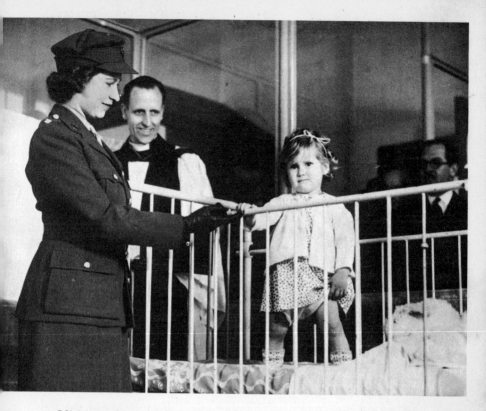

Visiting a hospital, Elizabeth tries to cheer up a sad little girl.

A lady-in-waiting is part secretary and part personal friend. She is a girl from a good family who goes nearly everywhere with the Princess, handles her pocket money, and sees that details are taken care of. The pay is very small. One of Elizabeth's ladies-in-waiting was married and ran her apartment without any hired help. She did her marketing on the way to work at the Palace. She arrived one morning on her bicycle with her market basket crammed with bundles and only a scarf covering her head. The Queen, looking out the window, said she thought the girl ought not to come to the Palace that way, especially without a hat. "Don't be old-fashioned, Mummie," Lilibet smiled. "These days girls simply don't *have* a hat."

Lilibet had a hat, though. In fact, she had quite a lot of them. They had to be chosen almost by rule. No matter what other people were wearing, the Princess had to have something that wouldn't hide her eyes or face from the crowds. Most of the hats had to be small and close-fitting, so she wouldn't have to go around clutching at them every time a breeze came up. The British people have very set ideas about how they expect royalty to look, and Lilibet always had to remember that.

Clothes were still rationed, because the long war had left Britain very poor and short of things for people to buy. All the same, Elizabeth simply had to have some new suits and dresses. She had got by with very few during the war, and most of the ones she had left were too "little girl." Lilibet had quite a womanly figure now. She was plumper, really, than she might have liked. But in Britain—where foods like meat and eggs and fruit still were hard to get—many people had gained weight on the starchy foods that were most plentiful.

This was the first time Elizabeth had ever thought much about clothes. For her first grown-up wardrobe she chose the kind of pastel garments—pretty but not very stylish—that women of the royal family had always worn. They went well, though, with her violet-blue eyes, her pink-and-cream skin and her softly curling light brown hair. For the country, of course, she had good British tweeds and sweaters. Lilibet used very little makeup. In her earlier 'teens she had experimented with some sultry, dark lipsticks, but her mother and Miss Crawford luckily were able to persuade her to settle for a fresher, more becoming shade.

Margaret mostly wore hand-me-downs from Lilibet. The younger Princess was much more clothes conscious, but she didn't really mind—except for the hats. Elizabeth was delighted when she found she could save ration coupons by having some of her mother's evening dresses made over.

The Heiress Presumptive's income was 6,000 pounds a year, the same as it had been since her father became King. Before the war this was about equal to $28,000. Now, with the British pound worth so much less in American dollars, it came to about $17,000 a year, or $325 a week. Out of this Lilibet had to pay for her clothes, her "household" staff, her personal entertaining, travel expenses and donations to church or charity. She could look forward to a "raise," though. When she turned twenty-one her income would go up to 15,000 pounds a year, or about $42,000.

Nobody could deny that Lilibet's "job" paid quite well. But it also had quite a few drawbacks. It was a little like being a "bird in a gilded cage," in the words of the old song. The Princess couldn't prowl around stores to window shop, and she couldn't even go for a casual walk around London. Except at Christmas time, dressmakers and shopkeepers brought everything to the Palace for her to try on and choose. Every place she went, police cleared a path for her. She would hardly have known how to cross a street in heavy traffic. Lilibet could do very few things on the spur of the moment. Her date book was made up for weeks and even months ahead.

* * *

Worst of all Elizabeth couldn't marry someone just because she had fallen in love. By now she and Philip were pretty sure that they were in love for keeps, but the husband of a future queen has to suit a lot of people. He has to please her father and mother, but he also has to please the Cabinet ministers, and even the people the queen will rule over. Some people thought Philip was rather "wild." He liked to roar around the roads in fast cars, and he had been known to smash them up a little. Philip wasn't a British citizen, either. Though he was a great-great-grandson of Queen Victoria, he was legally a Greek. In fact, he was fifth in the line of heirs to the Greek throne. And Britain and Greece hadn't been on very friendly terms since the war.

However, Philip had no Greek blood. He was Danish on one side of his family, English on the other. His father, Prince Andrew, was the younger son of King George of Greece, who was the son of King Christian IX of Denmark. Philip was born in Greece, on June 10, 1921, but his father and Princess Alice, his British mother, moved to France when he was a baby. Philip never saw Greece again until he was in the British Navy.

From the time he was a small boy he attended schools in England and Scotland. His mother's relatives became his legal guardians and his "family." His grandfather, the Marquess of Milford Haven, had been an admiral who became First Sea Lord of Britain. By 1938 Philip's guardian, as well as his hero, was another British admiral—his handsome uncle, Lord Louis Mountbatten. Lord Mountbatten commanded British and Allied forces in India and Southeast Asia during the war. Afterward, he was rewarded with the higher title of Earl Mountbatten of Burma, and was made Viceroy of India.

Philip could hope to be an admiral himself, someday. But if he became a Queen's husband, he would lose much of his freedom to make his own career and live his own way. He could hardly leave all the official duties to her while he stayed at sea.

If Philip worried about this, he must have felt that Elizabeth was worth it. He came to the Palace often to have supper with Lilibet and Margaret in the old nursery. Afterward they would have a romping game of ball in the corridors, or a quieter game of cards. Margaret always wanted to be part of her big sister's dates, but Philip would take just so much from her. In big-brother fashion he would tease her and take her down a peg or two when she put on too many fancy airs.

Lilibet didn't feel that Philip was "wild." She thought he was just informal, and a nice change from some of the stuffier people she had known. He had opinions of his own and said pretty much what he thought, and he looked at people directly and intensely with his deep-set blue eyes. Philip often wandered around Buckingham Palace in his shirt-sleeves or in flannel slacks and sport shirts.

After a time Elizabeth hardly went out socially unless Philip was going to be along. Miss Crawford felt she moped around her rooms entirely too much. But the Princess couldn't be happy until something was settled about her future. The King and Queen wanted Lilibet to be very sure of her feelings, so they invited Philip to go to Scotland with the family in August. Immediately the news was all over the British Isles that he and Elizabeth were engaged. It seemed, in fact, that almost everyone knew more about the Princess's plans than she did.

There was so much talk that, in September, the engagement was officially denied in a statement from Buckingham Palace. But Lilibet's close friends think to this day that she and Philip decided on their engagement while on a stag-hunt during the Scottish trip. If they did, it was their secret, because that autumn the Palace announced that Princess Elizabeth and her sister would accompany the King and Queen on an official visit to South Africa the next February.

* * *

Margaret really got excited over the trip. For one thing, she wouldn't have to do any lessons for a while. And for another, she was going to have almost her first chance to pick out a whole new wardrobe for herself. Lilibet faced the trip more as something that had to be done. She knew it would be interesting, and she did look forward to making the voyage on the great battleship *Vanguard*. She had a warm feeling for this ship because she had christened it in Scotland in 1944. But if people thought a long separation from Philip would change her mind about him, she knew they were wrong.

For a couple of days, Lilibet was very nearly seasick. But then she found her "sea legs," and the ship's officers gave the pretty Princesses a gay time. Under the South African sun, the royal family's special white train wound all over the country. They saw ostrich farms and gold mines, and were given "sparklers" by the handful at the South African diamond mines.

At a parade of Girl Guides in Basutoland Lilibet did one of those things that pleased everyone. She asked about a busload of Guides who were kept at a distance from the others. Someone told her they were children from a leper colony. Elizabeth promptly took Margaret and went over to the bus to chat with the girls through the open windows.

All during the four-month trip, Philip's picture was always on Lilibet's dressing table and she wrote him frequent letters. But she never forgot the main purpose of her life. In April, in the middle of the visit, she reached her twenty-first birthday.

A telegram from Philip was the first greeting she opened that morning. But before her birthday ball, in a broadcast heard all over the world, she dedicated herself to duty and her country.

"I declare before you all," she said, "that my whole life, whether it be long or short, shall be devoted to your service and the service of our great Imperial family to which we all belong. But I shall not have strength to carry out this resolution alone unless you join in it with me, as I now invite you to do. I know that your support will be unfailingly given. God help me to

The Princesses test their aim aboard HMS Vanguard enroute to Africa.

make good my vow and God bless all of you who are willing to share in it."

＊ ＊ ＊

Back home, as the *Vanguard* steamed into the harbor, those on board saw Princess Elizabeth do a little jig of joy. She knew that while the royal family was away, Philip's naturalization papers had come through. He had given up all claims to the Greek throne and was now a British subject. He had taken his uncle's name and was no longer Prince Philip but plain Lieutenant Philip Mountbatten of the Royal Navy. At last, thought Lilibet, something would surely happen!

Another six weeks dragged on, but Lilibet had a secret little glow about her. The King was informing the British Prime Minister, Mr. Clement Attlee, and the Prime Ministers of the British Commonwealth countries, that the engagement was about to be announced. They all assured the King of their approval. The last formality was over when a council of British officials met to hear the King's decision.

In the newspapers of July 9, 1947, the King announced the engagement of the Heiress Presumptive to her first and only love. Within a few hours 7,000 telegrams of congratulations had arrived at Buckingham Palace. The next day the King and Queen gave a garden party at the Palace for the happy couple. Lilibet kept stealing little glances at her engagement ring. It was a large, square-cut diamond with smaller diamonds on each side. Philip kept stealing little glances at Elizabeth.

＊ ＊ ＊

The wedding was set for November 20 in Westminster Abbey. Everybody was suddenly in a fever of plans and prep-

When the Queen lost a heel on rough ground in Africa, Lilibet gave her mother her own "saddles" and went on cheerfully in stocking feet.

Elizabeth and Philip are congratulated on their engagement.

arations, like nothing since the Coronation. Dressmakers brought sketches so Elizabeth could decide just how the royal wedding gown was to be made. The Queen and eighty-year-old Queen Mary unwrapped all the pretty fabrics they had been tucking away for years as a sort of "hope chest." Factories and stores all over the Commonwealth sent silks and linens and woolens. Old ladies sent heirloom laces that had been in their families for years. Shopgirls sent dainty handkerchiefs, and from Americans came hundreds of pairs of nylon stockings, which were not so plentiful in England.

By mid-autumn Buckingham Palace was a storehouse of

beautiful things, and the wedding presents were put on display. To raise money for charity, the public paid a small admission fee. They saw necklaces, bracelets, earrings and tiaras of diamonds, sapphires, emeralds and rubies. They saw four fur coats—a mink and a lustrous beaver from Canada, a mink jacket from Newfoundland, a soft gray evening cape of rare chinchilla from British fur-breeders. From South Africa came an evening cape of ostrich feathers dyed in one of Lilibet's favorite shades, lime green. There were delicate china and glassware and gleaming silver and handsome furniture. There was even a small sailing yacht, the *Bluebottle,* for Elizabeth and Philip from British yacht clubs. But that wasn't on display at Buckingham Palace!

Lilibet was overwhelmed. She felt almost guilty when she discovered that there was another bride-to-be at Buckingham Palace. Miss Crawford had been postponing her own marriage for a long time, because she felt the royal family needed her. Now, in September, she married her fiancé, who worked in a bank. She and Lilibet had a good laugh together when someone sent them an American newspaper with the headline: GOVERNESS BEATS LIZ TO ALTAR. The King gave Miss Crawford a small, charming cottage in London, with its own garden, to own for all her life.

The night before his daughter's wedding the King made another announcement. Philip would no longer be a British "commoner," or person without a title. The King was making him Duke of Edinburgh. This pleased the Scottish people immensely. The King also gave Philip the English title of Baron Greenwich and the Welsh title of Earl of Merioneth. Though his wife was a princess, Philip would not be a prince. But his father-in-law granted him the right to be called "His Royal Highness" anyway. The King also made Elizabeth and her bridegroom the youngest members of the Order of the Garter, the highest honorary order in Britain.

For the British people, the royal wedding day was a splash of color in a drab time of rationing, hard work and simple living. Neither laborers nor building materials could be spared to build special grandstands, inside Westminster Abbey or along the streets. So, instead of the 10,000 persons who had crowded the Abbey for the Coronation, there were a mere 2,500 wedding guests there. It was a public holiday only for school children, but outside the Palace and along the route to the Abbey, the crowd stretched almost as far as the eye could see.

Many of the spectators had camped in the streets over-night, cooking their breakfast on little camp stoves. So Elizabeth, on her wedding morning, awoke to whiffs of coffee and bacon drifting in through the open windows! On her own breakfast tray was a bouquet of white carnations from Philip.

The halls of Buckingham Palace were a-flutter with brides-maids. All eight were there to put on their frocks of white satin and tulle, and the wreaths of white flowers for their hair. In their white-gloved hands they would carry white orchids and lilies. The maid of honor, of course, was seventeen-year-old Margaret. The others were four cousins of Elizabeth's, two of her friends and one cousin of Philip's. Bobo dressed the bride, and Norman Hartnell, who had designed the wedding gown, was on hand to see that every detail was just right. Three hundred and fifty girls had worked seven weeks on the gown, stitching the thousands of pearls and crystal beads used to embroider it.

Meanwhile, at nearby Kensington Palace, Philip's dressing was a pretty simple matter. He had spent the night there, where his mother was a guest, after a gay bachelor dinner at

Here comes the bride! The coach carrying Elizabeth and her father
to Westminster Abbey is cheered by thousands in Trafalgar Square.

the Dorchester Hotel. Now he was putting on his dark blue Navy uniform, brightened with the gold stripe of a lieutenant and the rainbow of ribbons that stood for his Navy decorations. Below them he wore his new jewelled Star of the Order of the Garter. Below that was the Star of the Greek Order of the Redeemer. Like most other young Navy officers of these simple days, he had no sword of his own. He wore the sword of his grandfather, the Marquess of Milford Haven, the admiral who had been Britain's First Sea Lord.

Philip's best man was his cousin, the old admiral's grandson. He was the good-looking young Marquess of Milford Haven, a Navy lieutenant, too. Together, that morning, they drove to the Abbey in a royal car, behind an escort of motorcycle police. It made Philip feel happy about his future with the British people when the crowds cheered him and called out, "Good luck, Philip!" He gave them a big grin as he waved back.

Inside the mellow old Abbey, the organ played as the guests looked for their seats. It was a simply dressed gathering, compared with the elegance of the Coronation and pre-war royal weddings. Few people were in formal dress. There were, of course, nobles and their ladies, and Cabinet ministers, ambassadors, admirals, generals and representatives of the Commonwealth countries. But there were also Navy enlisted men who had served with Philip, corporals and sergeants from Elizabeth's Guards regiment, employes from Buckingham Palace and Windsor Castle and the Mountbatten home, girls who had worked on the wedding gown, and girls from the ATS. Members of Parliament had to draw straws to see who would get seats, since there weren't enough for all.

The audience kept its eyes on the great West Door. Through that door came most of Europe's last royalty — some who still had thrones and some who had lost them. There were the kings of Norway, Rumania, Denmark and Yugoslavia, and queens, crown princes and princesses from Greece, Belgium, The Netherlands, Spain, Luxembourg, and other countries.

Back at Buckingham Palace, a terrible last-minute flurry was going on. The bridal bouquet of white orchids was lost! High and low they hunted. Finally the flowers were found in a cooler. A footman had put them there to keep them fresh.

The bride's carriage was waiting.

Elizabeth walked through the double glass doors and down the red-carpeted steps. Her father, in admiral's uniform, handed her into the carriage and helped her arrange her billowing veil and train. Then they drove off behind high-stepping white horses. The cheer that went up became a solid roar that lasted from the Palace to the Abbey.

Ahead of the bride and her father rode Guardsmen on horseback. White and red feather plumes bobbed above their blue and scarlet full-dress uniforms. The Guardsmen were wearing these for the first time since the war had put the men into drab khaki. Bands played and blue and yellow banners, with the initials "E" and "P," rippled from flagpoles along the route.

Queen Elizabeth, in gold-flecked apricot brocade, and Queen Mary, in robin's egg blue velvet, had entered the Abbey with Philip's mother. They walked slowly to their seats up front, near the altar. For a moment Queen Elizabeth knelt in prayer. She must have thought, as she waited, of her own wedding to the tall young Duke of York in that very same spot.

The wedding ceremony was set for 11:30 A.M. Promptly at 11:28 Princess Elizabeth and her father entered the Abbey. They passed through an Army and Navy guard of honor, including eight girls in khaki from the ATS. The bells rang out as the great doors were thrown open. The organ music stopped. Trumpeters split the hushed stillness with the high, silvery, spine-tingling notes of a fanfare for Elizabeth, the bride. Every head turned as she came down the aisle, her left hand on her father's arm, while three choirs sang out together.

Elizabeth was a little pale. But a faint pink came and went in her delicate skin and her eyes were starry. Her bridal gown was of ivory satin, with a fitted bodice, long tight sleeves and a full skirt. What made it a fairy-tale dress was the pearl-and-crystal embroidery in a pattern of orange blossoms, York roses, star flowers and tiny ears of corn. From the sweetheart neckline, the skirt and the long train, the lustrous beading shimmered in the light of candles and the pale sun. Her veil was a foam of white tulle, held in place by a tiara of diamonds and pearls. She wore high-heeled, open-toe sandals of ivory satin, fastened with tiny silver buckles that were studded with pearls. Her train, of transparent ivory silk tulle, swept behind her for fifteen feet, heavy with the jeweled embroidery.

Carrying the train proudly were the bride's two five-year-old cousins, Prince William of Gloucester and Prince Michael of Kent. They wore white silk shirts and kilts in the Royal Stuart plaid. Behind the bride walked the eight bridesmaids. Princess Margaret, alone, was first, followed by eleven-year-old Princess Alexandra of Kent. As Elizabeth and the King passed each row of guests, the women dropped quick curtsies and the men bowed.

Elizabeth and Philip kneel as the Archbishop of Canterbury reads the vows.

The long walk down the aisle ended at the altar steps, where Philip waited with his best man. Behind Philip were the Archbishop of Canterbury, the Archbishop of York, and two other important clergymen. All of them were in the rich robes of the Church of England. Gold utensils shone on the high altar and white flowers banked it on either side. With her high heels and long train, Elizabeth looked taller than her five-feet-three-inches, even beside her six-foot husband. As the Archbishop of Canterbury read the vows, her answers were soft but clear. She promised to "obey" her husband as well as to love and honor him. Philip's answers were deep and firm. The King looked a little sad, as the father of the bride often does, but the Queen was calm and poised.

Then came the moment when Philip placed on his bride's finger the plain wedding band. It was made from a nugget of Welsh gold, as British royal wedding rings have been for generations. Perhaps the moment was too solemnly perfect. For as Elizabeth and Philip mounted to the high altar, attended only by Princess Margaret, the bride's train caught on the four steps. The little boys struggled manfully to free it, but with no success. Then Philip saw what had happened. He bent quickly and unhitched the train. All was well.

The bridal couple knelt in the Church of England manner, but Elizabeth had not forgotten the Scottish people. One of the hymns she chose for the wedding was the Scottish Presbyterian version of "The Lord Is My Shepherd." There were more prayers, scriptures and hymns—and then the final blessing. Amid a fanfare of trumpets and the singing of "God Save the King," the couple stepped into the chapel to sign the marriage register. Little Prince William tripped in his excitement, but Margaret caught him before he sprawled. Then came another fanfare, and the couple returned, moving down the aisle to Mendelssohn's Wedding March. As they reached the King and Queen, they paused, and the truly radiant bride gave every guest a memory to cherish. To her father and mother she made a deep, perfect court curtsy.

❊ ❊ ❊

The bridal couple were hardly back at Buckingham Palace before the crowds outside began to chant: "We Want Elizabeth and Philip!" Onto the balcony with them came their parents and their wedding party. Elizabeth was as pleased as the new Duke of Edinburgh when the people greeted the husband of their future queen with cries of "Good old Philip!"

Inside, 150 guests sat down to the wedding luncheon at fifteen tables centered with white carnations. At each place was a little bunch of white heather, sent from Balmoral, and a sprig of myrtle taken from a plant grown from a sprig out of Queen Victoria's wedding bouquet. Footmen in scarlet served the guests and five bagpipers from Balmoral marched around serenading them. But the three simple courses were all of unrationed food. The King proposed a toast to the bridal pair and the guests drank it in champagne. Elizabeth had received twelve wedding cakes as gifts. Using Philip's sword, the couple cut only the official cake—a four-tiered white one topped with a silver bowl of camellias and roses. The other cakes were sent to hospitals and institutions.

The early darkness of November had almost closed in when Lilibet ran down to the Palace courtyard in her going-away costume. It was a silk crepe dress and matching wool coat in the soft shade of powder blue called "love-in-the-mist." Her hat was a beret of the same blue with a feather cockade of darker blue. Philip took her by the hand and together they ran, laughing, to the carriage. Nobody threw rice at them—rice was rationed and people saved it for puddings!

But there was a snowstorm of paper rose petals from the luncheon guests. And the crowds, still waiting outside the Palace, were delighted when the Queen picked up her long silk skirts and—with the King—ran after the carriage to hurl a final handful of petals.

Lilibet had waited a long time to marry her Prince Charming. But now, at last, she was on her honeymoon. And before long, thanks to pictures like the one below, all the world could see how happy she and Philip were.

CHAPTER EIGHT

Parents and Travelers

IT WAS NEARLY A YEAR after the royal wedding, and the most interesting piece of furniture at Buckingham Palace was not the King's throne but a baby's bassinet. The same bassinet, in fact, that Lilibet and Margaret had used back in the old days at 145 Piccadilly. Now it was waiting for Lilibet's baby. It had been brought down out of one of the royal attics and made pretty and fresh again, all silk and lace ruffles. No blue-for-a-boy or pink-for-a-girl, though. Elizabeth and Philip didn't think a baby would feel very welcome if it arrived and found the wrong color. The royal bassinet was buttercup yellow.

It stood ready in the Palace nursery near Elizabeth's old apartment, which was now hers and Philip's. They had had a long, wonderful honeymoon, partly in England and partly at cozy little Birkhall in Scotland. For awhile, away from royal duties, they had almost been able to forget that they belonged to the British nation as well as to each other.

Then, like so many young couples after the war, they had come back to live with their in-laws. Philip went to work every morning at the Admiralty, the main office of the Royal Navy. It wasn't far from the Palace and usually he walked to work, though sometimes he drove off in his little sport-model car. In the evening Elizabeth watched at her window, waiting for him to come in sight. Then she would run down to meet him.

The King had given them a couple of royal houses, Clarence House in London and Sunninghill Park in the country, as wedding presents. Right in the middle of the re-modeling, Sunninghill burned to the ground. Some people said the fire had been started by "squatters"—families who had been bombed out of their homes and were sort of camping out where-ever they could find vacant property. Some of them may have been bitter because they felt they needed Sunninghill worse than the Princess and her husband. But Elizabeth just couldn't believe that anybody would burn it on purpose.

To take its place, she and Philip leased Windlesham Moor, a medium-sized house near Windsor. So while Elizabeth waited for her baby, she spent a lot of time with carpenters and painters and decorators. She got out the old knitting needles again, too. Knitting didn't seem like quite such a struggle when she wanted to make things for her own baby. The Princess got the same extra rations as other expectant mothers in England: a pint of milk a day, one-and-a-half times as much meat as other grown-ups and a bottle of cod liver oil every six weeks. She had all the eggs she could eat, from the royal hens at Windsor, and lots of her friends gave her their rations of oranges.

It was fourteen minutes past nine on Sunday evening, November 14, 1948, when Elizabeth's baby was born. "It's a boy!" was the news that went racing through the crowd waiting outside the Palace, practically under the new mother's window. And the guns at the Tower of London boomed 41 times to salute the Prince.

A young mother smiles down on her month-old son, Prince Charles.

The little Prince weighed seven pounds and six ounces. He was the first child born at the Palace since Queen Victoria's babies more than a hundred years before. Once again Britain had a boy child who would probably someday be King. His pleased young parents named him Charles Philip Arthur George. But to the public he was "Bonnie Prince Charlie," for the brave Scottish prince who was the hero of so many songs and stories. "From now on," said Princess Margaret, "I shall be known as Charlie's Aunt."

Elizabeth nursed her baby for the first three months of his life. Then she got measles. But within four months after he was born she was out opening bazaars, inspecting troops and visiting hospitals and factories. She and Philip made an official visit to Northern Island, and she made her third visit to Parliament to hear her old friend, Winston Churchill, in a debate on foreign policy. She dropped in, unannounced, at a London police court. For several hours she sat on the bench beside a woman judge who was hearing cases involving children. At lunch afterward, the Princess and the judge talked over something that had been worrying Elizabeth: the big postwar increase in juvenile delinquency.

When Prince Charles was eight months old, he and his parents finally moved into Clarence House, just down the Mall from the Palace. Elizabeth had fixed up a pretty nursery with cream-white walls, a soft blue carpet and draperies and slipcovers of cream chintz with red nursery-rhyme figures. Some of Lilibet's favorite old playthings were waiting for her son—toy soldiers and horses and teddy bears. Prince Charles had his own favorite toy, though. It was a big floppy, fluffy stuffed rabbit. It couldn't be found anywhere in Clarence House, and the little Prince set up a terrible howl. He didn't stop until his mother sent somebody back to get it at Buckingham Palace, where it had been left behind.

Elizabeth and Philip had a lot of fun getting their new house ready. It was big and old and they had furnished it mostly out of wedding presents and pieces the Royal Family already owned—which weren't always just what they would have chosen themselves. But by the time they got through it was fresh and charming and comfortable. The Princess had a sitting-room office done in her favorite shade of robin's egg blue with gay chintz upholstery, a pretty crystal chandelier and two strutting china roosters on the mantelpiece. Here she worked at her desk on speeches and letters. Philip had ideas, too, about how he wanted the first real home he had ever had to look. He brought home a lot of "gadgets" he had seen salesmen demonstrate when he went to a big fair.

With a family and homes of her own, Princess Elizabeth needed a bigger staff of employes. Lieutenant General Sir Frederick Browning, a Grenadier Guardsman who had commanded parachute troops during the war, was her business manager. He had charge of handling her income, paying her bills, running her homes and hiring and supervising her other employes. She had another man as her private secretary, two or three ladies-in-waiting and a Scotland Yard police inspector as a bodyguard. "Bobo" MacDonald was still Elizabeth's personal maid but there was a new "nanny" for Prince Charles. Philip had an "equerry," a sort of private secretary. He was a young Australian named "Mike" Parker, a lieutenant in the Royal Navy. He and Philip had been close friends ever since they served on destroyers together during the war. The Princess and the Duke liked to slip away to the London apartment of "Mike" and his wife for a simple supper and evening.

✳ ✳ ✳

Princess Elizabeth had barely reached twenty-one and the income of 15,000 pounds a year when her engagement was announced. To take care of her new life as a married woman, Parliament voted to increase this to 40,000 pounds a year—about $150,000. A few members of Parliament thought this was too much, when the country was so poor. But most of the British people seem to want the Royal Family to have enough money to live up to what the public expected of them. As King, Elizabeth's father received 410,000 pounds—well over a million dollars—a year. Most of it went to keep up a vast number of big homes, household staffs, yeomen of the Guard, traveling expenses, official entertaining and gifts to charity. All the "salaries" of British kings, queens, princesses, dukes and other royalty are paid out of the income from "Crown lands." These are city real estate or country acreage that earlier rulers acquired as the personal wealth of the Royal Family. They are still owned in the King's name, but these days he has to turn the income from them over to the government. Then the government, in turn, pays out to each member of the Royal Family whatever amount Parliament has decided on. When Parliament voted to give Princess Elizabeth 40,000 pounds a year, it also voted to give her husband 10,000 pounds a year of his own.

It was a good thing, too. For the Duke of Edinburgh's income as a Navy lieutenant was about $50—which shows why so few young Britons can afford to be officers unless they come from wealthy families. Even if the pay wasn't high, though, Philip's Navy career was important to him. He had hardly got his family settled at Clarence House before he started getting ready to go back to sea duty. In September, 1949, when Prince Charles was ten months old, Philip kissed his wife and

146

little boy good-bye and left to become First Lieutenant of the destroyer *Chequers*. The ship was based at Malta, a British island in the Mediterranean Sea between Italy and North Africa.

Elizabeth was now a real "Navy wife." And like many another Navy wife, she stood the separation as long as she could and then went off to join her husband. She stayed at Clarence House for the baby's first birthday party. Then she left him in the willing hands of his nanny, his Grandmother, the Queen, and his nineteen-year-old Aunt Margaret. She flew to Malta for a reunion with Philip on their second wedding anniversary, and she stayed several weeks. In the spring she flew down again to celebrate her twenty-fourth birthday with Philip. Before she went back to London they announced some good news: Elizabeth expected her second baby in August.

This time it was a little girl. Princess Anne Elizabeth Alice Louise was born at Clarence House August 15, 1950. She arrived the very day her father was promoted to Lieutenant Commander and she was just what he had said he hoped she'd be—"exactly like her mother." She had the same blue eyes and the same curly blonde hair Lilibet had as a baby. The Navy had given Philip a two-week leave for the baby's birth. When they sent him back to Malta, it was as captain of his own ship, the frigate *Magpie*. At last he was a full-fledged skipper!

Princess Anne's christening was in October. Like her brother Charles, she was christened at Buckingham Palace, wearing the same long ivory lace dress that he and Lilibet and all the royal babies had worn since Queen Victoria's time. Philip got home for that, too. But he had hardly gone back before he and Elizabeth decided being apart was no good. Off

Like any mother, Elizabeth finds two babies a handful.

to Malta she flew again. This time they went to Greece for a six-day visit with Philip's cousin, King Paul and his pretty young wife, Queen Frederika. Margaret came down to Malta for a week of Navy social life just before Christmas and Elizabeth stayed to spend the holidays with Philip. Their children were at Sandringham with the King and Queen.

When Elizabeth went home in February, she found some of the British newspapers—and a good many of the British people—were annoyed with her. They thought she was spending so much time with Philip that she was neglecting her children. Once before she had felt the sting of public criticism. In 1948, when she and Philip represented the King on an official visit to Paris, they went to a night club on Sunday. Strict church-goers in England and Scotland were terribly upset by this and called it "a dark day in our history." Most people, and the newspapers too, took the Princess's side. They

Two Scottish bagpipers discover that even a royal nose sometimes runs.

Parents and son sit still for a portrait but daughter goes exploring.

pointed out that she and the Duke had already been to church once that Sunday. Besides, the night club had been taken over by the British Embassy in Paris for a private party in the royal couple's honor.

But this time, in 1951, the criticism was more serious. Lilibet was really finding out how perfect the nation expected her to be—and how carefully she had to behave, if she wanted to please all of the people all of the time. She didn't know quite what she could do about it at the moment, though. Philip had a two-week leave coming up and they already had planned a visit to Italy. Maybe she also felt that she had as much right to be with her husband as anybody else. Anyway, after five weeks in England, she flew right back to Malta. She and Philip saw the sights of Rome and received guests at the British Embassy there. They also went to visit the Pope, Elizabeth wearing a long black dress with long sleeves and a black veil over her hair. This didn't please some of the church people back home either, since the Church of England split with the Catholic Church hundreds of years ago. Buckingham Palace had to explain that the Princess' visit was "private" and not official.

When she came home in April, right after her birthday, everyone expected that she would settle down. Almost at once, however, Buckingham Palace made another announcement: Princess Elizabeth and the Duke of Edinburgh would leave late in September for a five-week tour of Canada and a courtesy visit to Washington, D.C. Nobody criticized this trip. This was a royal duty. Elizabeth had found time to keep a few public engagements between her trips to Malta, but she spent most of her time with little Charles and Anne when she was home. Now, though, it looked as if she was starting back to work in earnest as a "career princess" as well as a wife and mother.

The King's health was not good, and Elizabeth began to take his place at more and more events. She was once again exactly the kind of future Queen the British wanted her to be when she appeared on horseback at the official King's Birthday.

Britain celebrates this in June, no matter when the monarch's birthday really is. This is so there will be a better chance of good weather for the holiday and the pageantry. The high spot is the "Trooping of the Color," a flag ceremony by the Brigade of Guards. Since the King was too ill to be present and "take the salute," Princess Elizabeth took it for him.

She rode out of the Buckingham Palace gates on a handsome big chestnut charger named "Winston," in honor of the wartime Prime Minister, Mr. Churchill. With graceful poise she rode side-saddle—something she had practiced for just such occasions. And as Colonel of the Grenadier Guards, she wore a feminine version of the Guardsmen's uniform. It was a scarlet military jacket with gold buttons and gold braid; a dark blue riding skirt, ankle-length; white gloves and a plumed, three-cornered hat of bearskin. This was an exact copy of the headdress worn by Colonels of the Guards two hundred years earlier. Some who watched had tears in their eyes. To them she was the symbol of Britain's historic glory and of the Royal Line that had never been broken in nearly a thousand years.

Her uncle, the Duke of Gloucester, rode beside her on a white horse down the Mall to the parade grounds. The Guardsmen marched and turned and marched again in a smart pattern. Then Elizabeth the Colonel rode forward to inspect the troops. Thousands of eyes followed her as she moved around the parade ground, erect and sure. But nobody watched more closely than a little boy in a sky-blue coat. Prince Charles thought the soldiers and the drums and the music were fine, but his mother was best of all. Back on the palace balcony the Princess, still in uniform, pointed up at the sky so her little boy wouldn't miss the jet airplanes flying overhead in honor of the King's Birthday.

Elizabeth represents her father at the "Trooping of the Color."

* * *

Philip came home in July. Some people predicted he would never go back to Navy service again, now that his wife needed help with her public duties. The King was somewhat better by August, so the whole family went up to Scotland as usual. But he caught a cold while shooting on the moors. It turned into pneumonia, and by late September the doctors had discovered that he had a serious lung disease and must have an operation.

His life was in danger. Almost at the last minute, Elizabeth and Philip had to postpone their trip to Canada. It was an anxious time for the whole British Commonwealth, and the whole world watched for news from the doctors at the King's bedside. After the operation, the King improved steadily—but Elizabeth was still worried about him. If he was no longer in real danger, though, she felt she had to go ahead with the tour. Canada was spending more than a million dollars on it. The schedule was all complete. To call it off would cause trouble to thousands of people. And her father, most of all, felt that she must go "on with the show."

Elizabeth had already flown more miles than any other royal person in history. Now she and Philip flew across the Atlantic Ocean. With them came a lady-in-waiting, Jean Elphinstone (while serving the Princess, she had met and married Lilibet's cousin, Andrew Elphinstone); "Mike" Parker, Lieutenant Colonel Martin Charteris, who was Elizabeth's private secretary, Inspector Kelley of Scotland Yard, "Bobo" MacDonald and two or three other servants.

The flying "royal coach" was a big blue-and-silver four-engine airplane. As it put down its wheels at the Montreal airport, Elizabeth's face was the only one that peered from the plane windows. She seemed eager as a small girl for her first glimpse of this New World—and perhaps a little anxious about how she would do. After all, this was the biggest assignment she had ever been given. But the Princess was a completely poised young woman as she greeted the Governor-General and the Canadian Prime Minister. Then she walked to a small, red-carpeted platform in the middle of the airstrip. She stood there, with Philip a few paces behind her, while a Royal

Canadian Air Force band played "God Save the King." Twenty thousand Canadians pressed against the airport fence to cheer their future Queen. When this reception was over, Elizabeth drove off to her special train to telephone her mother at Buckingham Palace and report that she and Philip were all right—and how were Papa and the children?

During the next five weeks the Princess and the Duke visited nearly a hundred towns and villages, with scarcely a moment to themselves except to sleep and change clothes. Their

In Ontario the Princess is greeted by the Dionne quintuplets.

"traveling palace" was a ten-car train. Elizabeth had a bedroom, dressing room and bath, with brown carpeting and pink taffeta and damask upholstery and draperies. Philip had a blue-and-white bedroom and bath adjoining hers, and their sitting room was paneled in birchwood.

There were a couple of tons of baggage for the royal party, including a matched set of red leather cases marked "H.R.H. Princess Elizabeth." People who saw the baggage put aboard the train noticed that the red cases were rather scuffed. There also were two huge wardrobe trunks—one marked "E" and the other "M." Elizabeth and Margaret had used them on their South African trip in 1947, and Elizabeth had borrowed her sister's trunk to bring to Canada.

At the towering Citadel of Quebec, where French cannon had fired on the British 200 years before, Elizabeth inspected a French-Canadian regiment that had made her its honorary colonel. She spoke in French to a mother whose two sons had died fighting with the regiment in Europe during the war. "*La Princesse* touched me twice on the hand," the woman said afterward, "and said, 'That's terrible—too much for one mother.'"

In Quebec, too, Canadian troops held a huge parade honoring Elizabeth on the Plains of Abraham. That was where the English General Wolfe had defeated the French General Montcalm in a great battle that won Canada for the British. To inspect the thousands of soldiers, Elizabeth rode among them standing up in a white-painted jeep, straight and steady in spite of the bumpy ground. She looked every inch a princess—a modern princess on a mechanical white charger.

That evening Elizabeth wore a full-skirted gown of silver

lace and tulle for the first of many state dinners she would attend in Canada. She made her speech in French. Before she stood up to give it, she pulled her compact out of her evening bag, stole a quick glance in her mirror, and hastily applied a little fresh lipstick. She held the mirror in her lap so other people at the table wouldn't see it. When she had finished her speech and sat down, Philip leaned across the Prime Minister of Quebec, who was sitting between them, and said something that could only have been "Well done!" or "Darling, you were wonderful." Elizabeth beamed back at him like a girl who had just made a hit as class valedictorian.

The royal train roared west to Ottawa, the Canadian capital. At a party there, given by Lord Alexander, the British Governor-General, Elizabeth and Philip went square-dancing, American-style. They found it just as much fun as Scottish reels. Looking through field glasses, they had their first glimpse of the United States as they stood on the Canadian side of Niagara Falls. The field glasses were the kind you have to pay a dime to see through. Philip rummaged through his pockets and then, grinning a little sheepishly, borrowed the dime from a local official who was pointing out the sights. From Windsor, Ontario, the royal couple saw the towering skyscrapers of Detroit, Michigan, just across the river—and thousands of Americans streamed across to the Canadian side to see them.

When they visited a children's hospital in Toronto, a small boy tried to take the Princess's picture and was nearly in tears because his camera wouldn't work. Elizabeth knelt down and told him: "I'll come back through this room a little later." By that time, he had borrowed another camera. He got his picture.

At a square dance in Ottawa Philip wears checked shirt and jeans . . .

...and Elizabeth sashays like a real country girl in a dirndl skirt.

Once, after the royal train had made one of its many ten-minute stops at a small town, the engineer started on his way again too soon—and left the Princess standing on the platform. While Elizabeth threw back her head and laughed, the crew managed to stop within a few feet. She and Philip each took a turn at riding up in the engineer's cab. In fact, the residents of Peers, Alberta, were startled to see Elizabeth pull into their station "driving" her own train.

The chief steward on the train revealed one of the royal couple's secret joys—orange juice! They reveled in the fact that oranges were more abundant than in England. They were likely to call for glasses of juice in their rooms at almost any hour. Unlike most travelers, Elizabeth never had to worry about her clothes. Faithful "Bobo" MacDonald spent a good many of her hours in Canada over an ironing board. Every morning she laid out three of the Princess's eighteen complete costumes, and Elizabeth chose the one that suited her mood.

The train rolled over the Canadian prairies and through the Rocky Mountains. The Princess and the Duke talked to Indians and cowboys, wheat farmers and lumberjacks, as her parents had done twelve years earlier. At Regina, Saskatchewan, headquarters of the Royal Canadian Mounted Police, scarlet-coated "Mounties" staged a musical horseback ride for them. Elizabeth, the girl who had always loved horses and good horsemanship, sat on the edge of her seat. She kept crying out "Oh, look!" and once she called out in warning to a rider when the saddle blanket slipped off his horse and caused another horse to shy and rear.

Nearly everywhere the local residents proudly served their finest, richest foods. One noon meal had food from ten provinces. It included, among other things, Nova Scotia

Locomotive No. 6057 gets a new engineer named Elizabeth.

oysters, Newfoundland salmon, Alberta elk meat, Saskatchewan grouse and Ontario cheese. "Is this a *luncheon*?" asked
the Princess, as if she couldn't believe it. She added, "If I ate
meals like this I would have to get a new wardrobe." Sometimes she barely tasted her food, but Philip usually pitched
into every dish like a man who needed nourishment and plenty
of it.

The "wild west" city of Calgary, Alberta, gave the royal
pair a change by serving them a cowboy "chuckwagon" lunch

of beef stew and beans. Elizabeth paused with a forkful halfway to her mouth to watch the children who were square-dancing for her, and then reached out to move a table lamp for a better view. Afterward, Elizabeth and Philip sat in a snowstorm, wrapped in electric blankets, to see a rodeo, and smilingly accepted gifts of ten-gallon hats. Philip wore his for the rest of the day. At another luncheon so many uninvited persons crowded in that the Princess and the Duke had to pass under an archway of creamed chicken—guests raised their plates high overhead to allow the royal couple to walk through the room!

The five-week schedule was so full that Elizabeth had trouble finding time to have her hair done. But in British Columbia she and her husband had a few days' vacation more or less to themselves. Tired of riding in back seats, they put the Scotland Yard man there instead and, with Philip at the wheel, drove a hundred miles to a hunting lodge in the woods of Vancouver Island. Philip got a big kick out of the car. It was a convertible roadster with white cowhide upholstery, a black and white calfskin floor covering—and two cowboy six-guns in holsters beside the driver's seat.

At a logging camp the royal couple watched "high climbers" cut the tops out of tall fir trees, and they went salmon fishing, as they often had in the River Dee in Scotland. Elizabeth relaxed in her favorite tweed suits and a head scarf the whole three days. She came back to start the trip eastward looking fresh and full of smiles.

All across the country the reporters and cameramen who traveled with the royal party were impressed with the huge crowds that came out to see the Princess and the Duke. Even at remote country crossroads, where the royal train only slowed down to let the Princess wave and smile, grown-ups and children had gathered from miles around. The tour was partly just a friendly "courtesy call" on the people of Canada. But Canada was prosperous and growing, and had been "feeling its oats" as a nation on its own. The newsmen knew that Princess Elizabeth was traveling partly to help bind Canadians closer to Britain and its other dominions.

To Canadians, the pretty, young Princess had some of the glamor of a movie star plus the patriotic importance of a President's visit. But she didn't have to run for office and she didn't have to work at being a "personality girl." The quiet, respectful crowds hadn't come to pick her to pieces with criticism. They seemed satisfied just to look at her, find her "prettier than we expected," and go away feeling pleased about their future Queen.

It was a strain for Elizabeth, of course, to have to be stared at so long and by so many people. There was a lot of stuffy, starchy routine to go through, too. Sometimes the young couple, surrounded by dignified older people, looked rather like a pair of youngsters trying hard not to wiggle in church. But Elizabeth, as Miss Crawford had once remarked, seemed to have "inborn, this desire to do what was expected of her." She didn't do very many impulsive things that would make the Canadians feel close to her, as a young girl they knew personally. But all her life she had been trained not to do things on the spur of the moment, without thinking of their effect. She was young and she was serious about her job, so she worked hard at not making any mistakes.

Traveling back across the country by train and plane, Elizabeth and Philip paused to see oil refineries, grain elevators and paper mills. They took color movies and they made almost daily telephone calls to Buckingham Palace—learning, during one, that little Princess Anne had taken her first steps. On a raw, bitter day at a Royal Canadian Air Force station, they met a young Englishman who had been sent over for training with the RCAF. He was embarrassed by his chattering teeth as he tried to talk to the Princess. "I'm just getting used to a Canadian winter, ma'am," he stammered with a grin. Said Elizabeth, who had been through snow, rain and gales during her trip: "It takes a bit of getting used to."

* * *

On October 31 Elizabeth and Philip flew down to Washington, D.C., to spend two days as the guests of President and Mrs. Truman and their daughter Margaret. They had already met Margaret in England. Elizabeth seemed to sense that she could relax more in a country where she was just an attractive visitor and not a Queen-to-be. And she must have really felt that things were different in the United States when photographers shouted to the President that they wanted "just one more shot" of him and the Princess together. In a fatherly manner, Mr. Truman said to the Princess: "Stand over here, dear."

Elizabeth and Philip went to Mount Vernon to lay a wreath on the tomb of George Washington, who had led his countrymen in revolt against the British. At the Library of Congress they saw the original copy of the Declaration of Independence. Philip, peering at it curiously, asked: "Does it really say 'Taxation without representation is tyranny'?" They presented Mr. Truman an antique gold-framed mirror and a pair of candlesticks as a gift for the White House.

When the President proposed a toast to Elizabeth at a

dinner party, he said she was just the kind of "fairy princess" he had dreamed of as a boy in Missouri. "We have many distinguished visitors here in this city," he said in a speech at the White House, "but never before have we had such a wonderful young couple that so completely captured the hearts of all of us." At a party at the British Embassy Elizabeth and Philip shook hands with more than a thousand Americans, including a Boy Scout in uniform, the national president of the Girl Scouts, and a 4-H Club girl.

Americans and Canadians alike found that Princess Elizabeth was smaller and prettier than her pictures seemed to show. She had a kind of shimmer that came from health, good grooming and poise. She had the good posture and nice manners that every mother wants for her daughter—and that every girl one day wishes she had. The Princess was not always smiling and relaxed. Sometimes she looked tired and a little bored and even nervous. But always Philip was there, to please the crowds with his big grin and hearty wave. He stood nearby, always in his proper place a few steps behind Elizabeth, beaming with pride when she had made a good speech or ready to give her a word of suggestion or encouragement. When he did have suggestions, Philip didn't bother with formality. To Her Royal Highness he just whispered urgently, "Betty!"

Philip could take some of the credit for Elizabeth's new figure. He had teased her into going on a diet. Though she still had curves, she was slim and tiny-waisted now. He had ideas about how he liked his wife to dress, too. With his help she had broken away from rather flowery styles. Now her daytime clothes were elegantly simple, well-tailored and striking. She wore cherry reds, deep greens, rich silvery blues. She used no eye make-up or bright nail enamel, though she used nail polish in a natural shade or a soft pink. She did not smoke, at least in public, and she drank no liquor. Sometimes at parties she drank a glass of champagne or some other wine, but when she had her choice she usually took orange juice.

Thousands of Americans saw the Princess on television. But the Princess didn't see as much of the United States as she wanted to. She had hoped, especially, to visit New York. To the very last she thought maybe her plane could dip low over the city, if only for just a glimpse. But when she flew over New York, on her way back to Canada, there was too much fog.

Again the royal train rolled out of Montreal, this time toward Eastern Canada, where the Maritime Provinces welcomed Elizabeth as "the daughter of a sailor and the wife of a sailor." Philip, in fact, had visited Halifax on one of his ships during the war. Taking tea there at a private home, Elizabeth sat on the arm of a sofa. When the hostess asked her if she wouldn't like a more comfortable seat, she smiled: "No, I like to perch."

The Princess and the Duke visited Prince Edward Island, famous to at least three generations of girls as the scene of the book, "Anne of Green Gables." The Islanders gave Elizabeth a specially-bound edition of the book to take back to the small Princess whose name, also, was Anne.

At Saint John, New Brunswick, as the couple returned to their train in high spirits after a dinner party, Elizabeth did a few little dance steps and curtsies toward the waiting crowd. She and her husband took several smiling "curtain calls" on the rear platform of their car. The delighted crowd continued to cheer and call for them. Finally Philip threw up the window blinds, shut the door, turned out the lights with elaborate gestures, and did everything to show the evening was over.

They sailed from Newfoundland on November 12 on the big Canadian ocean liner, "Empress of Scotland." To reach their ship, they had to board a small boat that was pitching like a nutshell in the high waves of a violent storm. Villagers sang the folk songs of Newfoundland fishermen above the crashing sea, and the local women made their farewell curtsies on a watery, lurching deck. Elizabeth, with a beige rain cape over her mink coat, kept a fairly even keel. Philip, steady on his feet as only a sailor could be, grinned his delight with the whole thing. When the hour-long, careening trip to the liner was over, Elizabeth had proved she was a good sailor. While others looked a little green, she boarded the big ship and said cheerfully to the captain, "Let's have lunch right away."

By the time London welcomed them back, they had traveled more than 18,000 miles by train, plane, automobile and ship. And already it had been announced that soon they would start out again! They would go half way around the world to Australia and New Zealand for five months. The trip had been planned for the King and Queen and Princess Margaret until the King fell ill. Elizabeth and Philip would go instead—but not until after Christmas.

On his birthday in November of 1951, Prince Charles tells his grandfather, King George VI, how it feels to be three years old.

CHAPTER NINE

Elizabeth the Queen

IT WAS A CHRISTMAS that broke all records. The King's health was improving and Elizabeth relaxed happily, enjoying this time with her parents and her sister and her children. From Canada she and Philip had brought back many presents they had been given. For little Prince Charles and Princess Anne there were Indian costumes and cowboy shirts, handknit sweaters, maple sugar, a knitted red Santa Claus doll, a little electric auto that ran under its own power and hundreds of other exciting packages — some of them to be put away carefully for later years. There were stories to tell about Canada and the United States, stories that brought other stories from the King and Queen as they went back in memory to their own Canadian trip. On January 30, the night before Elizabeth and Philip were to leave again, the Royal Family gave a theater party for them. They all went to see the American musical play, *South Pacific*. The King looked thin and haggard, but he was cheerful and proud of his daughter and son-in-law.

The next day he was at the airport to see them off, along with Prince Charles and Princess Anne and the rest of the family. Elizabeth had a special smile and wave (and perhaps a lump in her throat) for her father as she and Philip got into the big plane and took off into the cold air. Their first stop would be Africa.

It was sunny and warm when they landed in the British colony of Kenya. In summer clothes Elizabeth got busy on a round of official engagements. Then she and Philip went for a few days' vacation at a hunting lodge. It was their wedding present from the people of Kenya and they had never seen it before. Deep in the tropical jungle, they spent a night in a tree-house, taking pictures of wild animals as they came to drink at a water-hole. The next morning, February 6, they were up before dawn. They watched a fight between two rhinoceroses. They tossed bananas to baboons. They walked within ten yards of a herd of wild elephants before reaching the safety of a ladder to the tree-house. Then they returned to the main lodge.

It was lunchtime there when "Mike" Parker, listening to the radio, heard the terrible news—the King was dead! In a telephone call to London, Colonel Charteris confirmed that it was true. They told Philip first. He took his wife down beside a little stream and gently broke the news to her, the girl who had been Her Royal Highness and now was Her Majesty, Queen Elizabeth. For a little while she cried in his arms. Then, according to people who were at the lodge with her, "she took it like a Queen." She sent messages by cable to her mother and Queen Mary. She sent other cables to Australia and New Zealand and remembered to thank everyone who had been kind to her in Kenya. Then she prepared to return home at once.

She was the first Queen of Britain to inherit the crown in 115 years, since the accession of the dignified, very proper Victoria. At the moment Elizabeth became Queen, she was

This is the "Treetops Hotel" in Africa where the royal couple were photographing wild animals at the moment Elizabeth became Queen.

perched in a tree-house, wearing brown slacks and yellow shirt—and shooting movies. Now she took off from a modern airport on a continent that in Victoria's day was "darkest Africa." Flying over the Alps, she sat with the pilot and took more pictures, calming herself and those around her with this every-day hobby.

It was dusk when the plane reached London. Officials were lined up at the airport to greet their new monarch. One face, especially, she was glad to see. It was Winston Churchill's. He had first served his country in the Army, under Victoria. Now, at seventy-seven, he had been voted back into office as Prime Minister. Rows of the new Queen's subjects, silent and bare-headed, lined the roads for miles as she and Philip drove to Clarence House. Queen Mary was waiting. She made a deep curtsy to her granddaughter, who was now her Queen.

The next morning, at St. James's Palace, Elizabeth took the oath as Queen. She was dressed in black for mourning, with a heavy veil. To the nobles and officials who were gathered, she said: "I pray that God will help me to discharge worthily this heavy task that has been laid upon me so early in my life." Four trumpeters stepped to the balcony and blared out a fanfare. To the ancient ritual of proclamation, a micro-phone had been added. Heralds took their place as the Garter King of Arms, in a cockade hat and the historic costume of a knight, proclaimed: "The high and mighty Princess Elizabeth Alexandra Mary is now become Queen Elizabeth the Second. God Save the Queen."

Crowds took up the cry, guns boomed and the procession of gilded coaches moved off to proclaim the news at four other places in London. Elizabeth, back at Clarence House, watched the ceremonies on television.

The King of Arms proclaims Elizabeth the Queen of England

Now she was free to go to Sandringham to be with her mother and Princess Margaret. For the ride through the countryside, only a scarf crowned Elizabeth's hair, schoolgirl fashion. The Duke of Edinburgh was in the driver's seat, but his wife was Queen of England.

The King's body was brought back to London, where 300,000 persons stood in line to pass the coffin as it lay in state in Westminster Hall. The bells of Westminster Abbey tolled as the coffin was placed on a gun carriage to begin the trip to Windsor Castle for burial. Two million persons lined the route.

A gun-carriage bears the body of King George VI to its final resting place.

Behind the coffin rode Queen Elizabeth II and the King's widow, now the Queen Mother, in a coach pulled by two white horses. Following on foot were the Duke of Edinburgh, the Duke of Gloucester, the boy Duke of Kent (nephew of the King) and the Duke of Windsor, Lilibet's "Uncle David." He had flown from New York for the funeral. In a window of Marlborough House, Dowager Queen Mary raised her hand in a broken gesture of farewell to her son.

In a vault at St. George's Chapel, at Windsor Castle, King George VI was laid to rest with earlier members of his family.

On the casket lay a fragrant white wreath of camellias, carnations, lilies of the valley and hyacinths. The card said: "Darling Papa, from your loving and devoted daughter and son-in-law, Lilibet, Philip."

✻ ✻ ✻

The Queen named Elizabeth is the fortieth monarch of an unbroken line to reign over Britain. She is the sixth Queen to rule there in her own right. The Crown has lost power, even since Victoria's time, but it has gained in affection and has become even more important as a symbol. For the Crown is the one official link that unites all the people of the British Commonwealth's dominions and colonies. The realm of Queen Elizabeth II covers one-quarter of the earth's surface. Her subjects number more than half a billion.

Elizabeth became Queen at a period when "abnormal" times had come to seem the normal way of life. British troops were fighting in Korea and Malaya. The British people, tired of "doing without" during the long war, had just been told by Mr. Churchill that they would still have to "do without" some more. Britain disagreed with Russia on many things, and a big share of the nation's wealth was to be used to build up a strong Army and Navy.

In this difficult time, the young Queen shone as the one bright emblem of British unity, historic glory and future hope. A woman on the throne reminded the British, too, of the great days of earlier Queens—especially the first Elizabeth and Victoria and her husband, Albert. During his lifetime, Victoria had leaned on her husband for help in every decision she had to make. Albert, in turn, had devoted himself entirely to helping his wife carry the burden of her duties. But Albert was solemn and dignified and he had given up no special career of his own. Philip was independent and outspoken and he could have expected a brilliant Navy career in his own right.

As Elizabeth went to work at being Queen, however, she seemed to have a real partner in her husband. The Duke was president of the British Association for the Advancement of Science. He was chancellor of the University of Edinburgh and the University of Wales. They were honorary jobs but he turned them into a real interest in the progress of science and education. He made many speeches, sometimes taking Elizabeth's place, and he wrote all his speeches himself.

As the time of his wife's formal coronation drew nearer, the Duke was a busy member of the commission making the plans. Now Elizabeth announced officially that he was the "First Gentleman of Britain." Until then his little son, as heir to the throne, had ranked above him. It looked, too, as if Philip would have his own "ship" after all. Through the Admiralty, Elizabeth ordered the first sea-going yacht the Royal Family had built in fifty-three years.

* * *

As a ruling queen, Elizabeth had to do both the things her father had done as King and the things her mother had done as Queen and wife. This took some planning. She told Mr. Churchill he would have to change the hour when he usually came to report on government matters. From 5:30 to 6:30 in the evening was a time she spent with her children, and she was not going to change that. She was at her desk by 9 or 9:30 every morning, doing "paperwork." She spent another two or three hours there after lunch if she had no public engagement.

In May of 1952 Elizabeth and her family moved back into Buckingham Palace. The Queen Mother and Princess Margaret remained there, too, at least for the time being. But it was Elizabeth who was now head of the household. She had 250 office staff members and hundreds of servants, instead of the ten she had at Clarence House. She remembered the chilly old days in the Palace and refused to go through the same thing again. She had an oil burner installed to heat the family apartments. Steam heat was piped into the Throne Room and big, elegant Green Drawing Room—which she had done over in ivory. She couldn't do all she would like to, though, even if she was one of the richest women in the world, with castles and land and cars and horses in her name and Crown Jewels alone worth $80,000,000. She still had to economize in order to meet all of her royal obligations. To cover these, Parliament raised her "allowance" to 475,000 pounds (about $1,300,000) a year. It gave Philip another 40,000 pounds annually ($110,000).

The official period of mourning for her father ended May 31. In June, Elizabeth held her first "courts." At each one five hundred debutantes made their curtsies to the Queen and the Duke. Ten American girls were among them. Princess Margaret stood beside her sister and both of them had memories— of two little sisters, in quilted pink dressing gowns, who had hung out the window on court nights to watch the glamorous debutantes arrive to be presented to the King and Queen. In July the new Queen held her first two garden parties, with 7,000 guests at each one. One of the guests was Margaret Truman.

The formal Coronation of Queen Elizabeth II was set for

June 2, 1953. Many visitors from overseas were coming, the Coronation was a world event. Britain was in a fever of preparation. Westminster Abbey had been closed since Easter, 1952, so workmen could get it ready. They built extra seats, shined up the lovely old carvings and stained glass and laid down carpets specially designed for the occasion. Fashion designers took the Coronation as the theme for their styles, choosing "royal" colors of rich reds, blues and purples. A famous composer was writing a special opera to be given at the Royal Opera House as a Coronation event. Newsmen prepared to broadcast, photograph and write about the ceremonies. Nobility and commoners were already planning what they would wear. Many a peer and peeress, so poor these days they had sold their finery for cash, would attend the Coronation in rented robes. And in the Tower of London the Crown Jewels were taken out of their display cases, to be ready to gleam and flash on the great day.

The center of it all would be Elizabeth. Philip would be near her and her mother and the baby prince and princess would watch proudly. But only Elizabeth would have the three-hundred-year-old crown placed on her head. Elizabeth, the girl who loved and was loved by her countrymen, her family and her husband—but who must stand alone in her own unique job. "Look at Lilibet, there," her father had said once as he saw her by herself in the center of a respectful crowd. "Poor, lonely girl. She'll be lonely all her life."

❊ ❊ ❊

She looked, though, like a young woman who had found pride and pleasure in her role as she performed the first great state ceremony of her reign. This was on November 4, 1952,

Elizabeth the Queen enters the House of Lords on the arm of the Duke of Edinburgh to open the meeting of Parliament.

when she opened Parliament with the traditional Speech from the Throne.

Noble peers who make up the House of Lords, elected members of the House of Commons and diplomats from all over the world crowded into the House of Lords chamber to await the young Queen's arrival. Peers in scarlet and ermine sat on steps or in the aisles. Judges and Parliamentary officials were there in wigs and gowns. Some peeresses wore tiaras and glittering dresses. Others, in felt hats and fur coats, looked as if

179

they had merely taken an hour or so off from the workaday world.

With her husband beside her, Queen Elizabeth drove out of Buckingham Palace in the handsome Irish State Coach. As they left the courtyard, Prince Charles and Princess Anne waved from a Palace window. Guardsmen on horseback rode down the Mall ahead of the carriage, and a salute of 41 guns thundered above the noise of London traffic.

As Elizabeth entered the House of Lords, everyone stopped talking. In silence she walked through the chamber with Philip beside her, escorting her by the hand. Her gold lace dress hugged her tiny waist under a wide, tight belt. Her crimson velvet train, borne by two pageboys, and her diamond jewelry had been worn by her great-great-grandmother, Queen Victoria. Because Elizabeth had not yet been crowned officially, she wore a coronet of diamonds and pearls. It was the first time a Queen had opened a session of Parliament since 1886, when Victoria last visited the House of Lords. And when the Duke of Edinburgh had conducted his wife to the huge gilt throne, he quietly took the simple chair beside it. This was where Prince Albert had sat when his wife, Victoria, made her speeches.

Carrying the Sword of State was Lord Alexander, the British Minister of Defense—the same man who, as Governor General of Canada had taught this regal young woman to do American square dances a year earlier. "My Lords, pray be seated," said the Queen. The bewigged Lord Chancellor, on bended knee, held up a scarlet velvet cushion. On it was a scroll of parchment. Elizabeth took it and began to read the Speech from the Throne.

She told Parliament how grateful she was for the sympathy

*On the Palace balcony where she first appeared as a child,
Elizabeth Regina and her own family salute the British people.*

expressed "from every part of the Commonwealth" after
King George VI's death. "By his selfless devotion to his duties
as your sovereign," she said, "my father set an example which
it will be my constant endeavor to follow." She said, too, that
late in 1953 she planned to leave again on her interrupted trip
to Australia, New Zealand and Ceylon "in company with my
dear husband."

Queen Elizabeth told the lawmakers of her hope for an
early armistice in Korea and of "my Government's whole-
hearted attachment to the ideals of the United Nations." She
spoke of the plans of "my ministers" to work closely with the
nations of Western Europe, South America, and the United
States. She spoke, too, of the plans of "my Government" to
return to private owners the steel and transport industries of Brit-

ain. The Labor Party had made them national property after the war.

The words were those of Prime Minister Winston Churchill and his Cabinet ministers of the Conservative Party. But the fresh, clear voice was the voice of the young, modern Queen—daughter of a royal line that had worn the British crown for nearly a thousand years. Elizabeth Regina! Elizabeth the Queen. Her role would be to make her queenship a symbol that would unite and inspire her people. Already, with her Coronation still to come, Elizabeth the Queen had given Britain a glorious moment to add to its history.

PHOTOGRAPHIC CREDITS

COMBINE: front jacket, back jacket, title page and pp. 8, 21, 27, 35, 39, 57, 73, 93, 98, 105, 121, 127, 130, 148, 150, 158, 168, 173, 174, 179, 181

UNITED PRESS PHOTOS: pp. 14, 19, 29, 37, 46, 48, 85, 103, 109, 137, 159, 161, 183

INTERNATIONAL NEWS PHOTOS: pp. 7, 43, 51, 65, 82, 91, 114, 129, 133, 140, 143, 149, 153, 155

KEYSTONE: pp. vi, 11, 24, 32, 45, 63, 67, 68, 171

WIDE WORLD: p. 69

BOOKS CONSULTED:

ACLAND, ERIC. *The Princess Elizabeth.* John C. Winston Company, Ltd. Toronto, 1937.

ASQUITH, LADY CYNTHIA. *The King's Daughters.* Hutchinson and Company Ltd. London.

BATCHELOR, VIVIEN. *Her Most Gracious Majesty, Queen Elizabeth II.* Pitkins, London.

BATCHELOR, VIVIEN. *T.R.H. The Princess Elizabeth and the Duke of Edinburgh and Their Children.* Pitkins, London.

BRADLEY, OMAR. *A Soldier's Story.* Henry Holt and Company, New York, 1951.

CHANCE, MICHAEL. *Princess Elizabeth and Her Dogs.* E. P. Dutton and Company, New York, 1937.

CRAWFORD, MARION. *The Little Princesses.* Harcourt Brace and Company, New York, 1950.

CRAWFORD, MARION. *Elizabeth the Queen.* Prentice Hall Inc., New York, 1952.

LIFE's *Picture History of World War II.* Simon and Schuster, New York, 1950.

PEACOCK, LADY IRENE. *Her Majesty Queen Elizabeth II, Her Life of Service as Princess Elizabeth*. Hutchinson, London.

PEACOCKE, MARGURITE D. *The Pictorial Story of Buckingham Palace* AND *The Pictorial Story of Windsor Castle*. Pitkins, London.

SHERIDAN, LISA. *Princess Elizabeth and Princess Margaret Rose at Home*. E. P. Dutton, 1941.

TOWERS, FRANCES. *The Two Princesses*. National Sunday School Union, The Pilgrim Press, London.

A King's Story, Memoirs of the Duke of Windsor. G. P. Putnam's Sons, New York, 1951.

WULFF, LOUIS. *Queen of Tomorrow*. Sampson Low, Marston and Company, Ltd. London.

PERIODICALS CONSULTED:

Files of THE NEW YORK TIMES, 1926–1952.

LECLER, RENE. "England Prepares to Crown a Queen," COSMOPOLITAN Magazine, October, 1952.

Cover Story, Queen Elizabeth II. LIFE Magazine, February 18, 1952.

Cover Story, Queen Elizabeth II. TIME Magazine, February 18, 1952.

WINOCOUR, JACK, "Philip, Duke of Edinburgh," (two articles) LIFE Magazine, October, 1951.

Cover Story, Princess Margaret. NEWSWEEK Magazine, August 18, 1952.

BOCCA, GEOFFREY, "Queen Elizabeth, the World's Busiest Mother," THE SATURDAY EVENING POST, November 8, 1952.

Stories on the Opening of Parliament by Queen Elizabeth II. THE TIMES of London, November 3, and November 5, 1952.

26 5163